PERCEPTUAL
PUZZLERS

THUNDER BAY
P · R · E · S · S
San Diego, California

Thunder Bay Press

An imprint of the Advantage Publishers Group

5880 Oberlin Drive, San Diego, CA 92121-4794

www.thunderbaybooks.com

ISBN 1–59223–019–9

Printed and bound in China

2 3 4 5   09 08 07 06 05

erceptual Puzzlers is a fun and challenging collection of brainteasers for anyone who wants to get a new angle on their 3-D skills or the geometry behind games of shape. There is plenty for everyone in this collection, as the puzzles require different levels of skill and amounts of time to complete.

Most of the skills you'll be using on these puzzles come from the right-hand side of your brain, which controls the left-hand side of your body. Right-hemisphere skills include gestalt (insight, the ability to see the big picture), 3-D formations, awareness of color and shape, musical talent, imagination, and (believe it or not!) daydreaming.

Our perceptual skills are not as consciously tested as vocabulary or mathematical abilities. Being able to squeeze your car through a tight space or work out which key fits your front door are just two examples of how our everyday unconscious uses visual cognition. Despite the obvious practical applications, there is something unnerving about testing these skills—it seems that without the comfort of words and numbers to help us, we are in a different world where we have to look beyond the obvious. Colors, spacing, lines, corners, directions, and arrangement could all have an effect on the answer—but which ones are relevant?

The trick, therefore, is to look beyond the illustrations and focus on the principles being employed. Don't let the abstract shapes and unfamiliar patterns fool you, for the principle behind each and every puzzle here is relatively straightforward.

Our crack team of puzzle-constructors has carefully crafted a spectacular range of challenges. Not all the obstacles around this course are the same. The star grading assigned to each puzzle in the book tells you what kind of territory to expect—a low number of stars indicates that you're on the bunny slope. But if you're tackling an eight-, nine-, or ten-star problem, expect to get your crampons and pickax out, for these are the hardest of all. Each puzzle has also been given a time target rating as well, so you've got to keep an eye on the clock. However, keep in mind that both difficulty ratings and target times are based on an average performance, so don't be surprised if you sail through a ten-star puzzle or find yourself struggling with a three-star—everyone is different.

So have fun while rolling dice, completing sets, toppling dominoes, tracking through the mazes, and spotting those differences. If you think help is needed, the answers section is on constant standby. Every question is numbered and has its answer clearly marked in the back of the book. But be sure to try all avenues before resorting to the solutions—things are not always what they seem at first!

With patience and practice, by the end of *Perceptual Puzzlers*, you'll be looking at the world in a whole new light ○

—Alison Moore

1 DIFFICULTY ✪✪✪✪✪✪✪✪✪✪

Target time: 5 minutes

Find your way from the front of the house to the back.

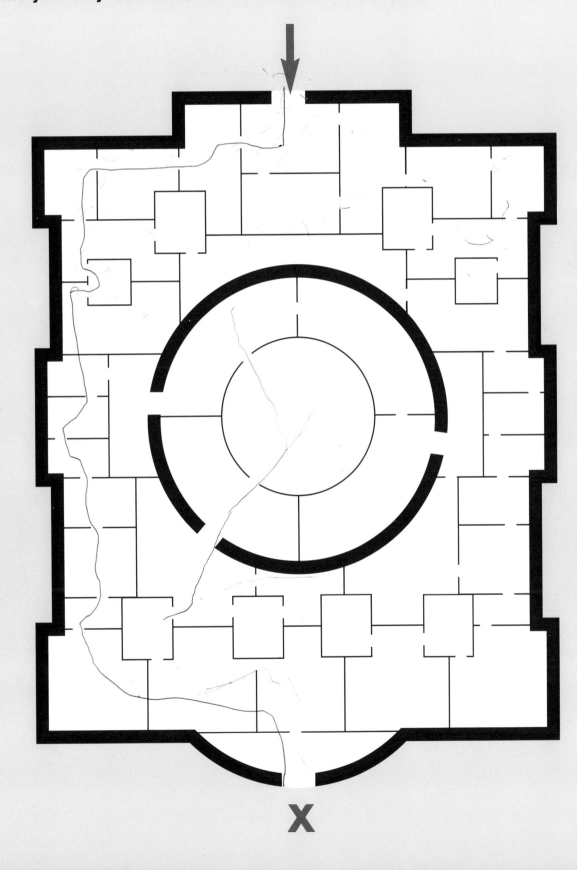

X

2 DIFFICULTY ✪✪✪✪✪✪✪✪✪✪

Target time: 5 minutes

This is a two-player game. Players take turns removing either one coin or two touching coins. The winner is the person who picks up the last coin. Once you've played the game a few times, see if you can work out how to guarantee a win if your opponent plays first.

3 DIFFICULTY ✪✪✪✪✪✪✪☆☆☆
Target time: 5 minutes

Study the shapes below for one minute, then see if you can answer the questions on page 10 without checking back.

4 DIFFICULTY ✪✪✪☆☆☆☆☆☆☆
Target time: 3 minutes

Can you spot the eight differences between these two pictures? Circle them in the drawing on the right.

[3] DIFFICULTY ✪✪✪✪✪✪✪✩✩✪

Target time: 5 minutes

Can you answer these questions about the puzzle on page 9 without checking back?

1. How many Ms are white? *2*
2. How many Es are dark gray? *1*
3. How many Hs are white? *0*
4. How many Ks are purple? *0*
5. How many Ks are there in total? *3*
6. What is the total of yellow Ks plus yellow Es? *3*
7. What is the total of blue Hs plus purple Zs? *2*
8. What is the total of all letters except Es? *2*

5 DIFFICULTY ✪✪✩✩✩✩✩✩✩✪

Target time: 2 minutes

Three dice were placed on a glass coffee table to amuse baby Adam, crawling underneath. Adam can see only the bottom faces of the dice. If he could count, what is the total number of spots he'd say he can see?

6 DIFFICULTY ✪✪✪✪✪✪✪✪✪✪

Target time: 30 minutes

You may want to run as far away as possible from this nonogram!

HOW TO DO A NONOGRAM:

Along each row or column, there are numbers that indicate how many blocks of black squares are in a line. For example, "3, 4, 5" indicates that from left to right or top to bottom, there is a group of three black squares, then a group of four black squares, then another group of five black squares.

Each block of black squares on the same line must have at least one white square between it and the next block of black squares. Blocks of black squares may or may not have a number of white squares before and after them.

It is sometimes possible to determine which squares will be black without reference to other lines or columns.

It is helpful to put a small dot in a square you know will be empty.

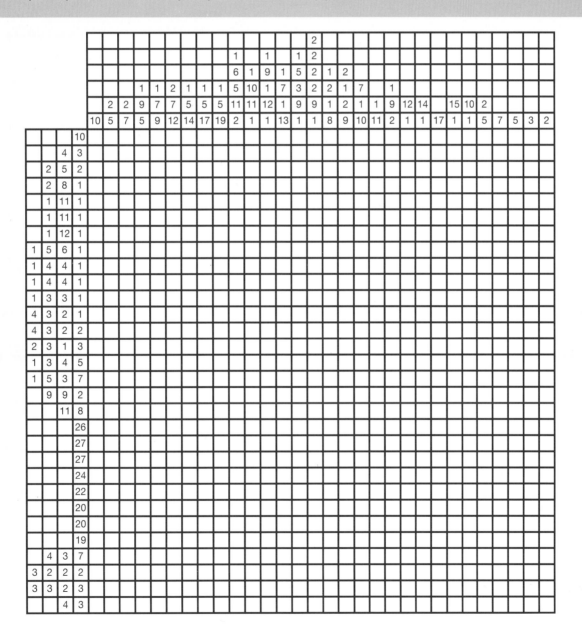

DIFFICULTY ✪✪✪✪✪✩✩✩✩✩
Target time: 6 minutes

Find your way to the center of the maze.

8 DIFFICULTY ✪✪✪✪✩✩✩✩✩✩
Target time: 3 minutes

Which of the four boxed figures completes the set?

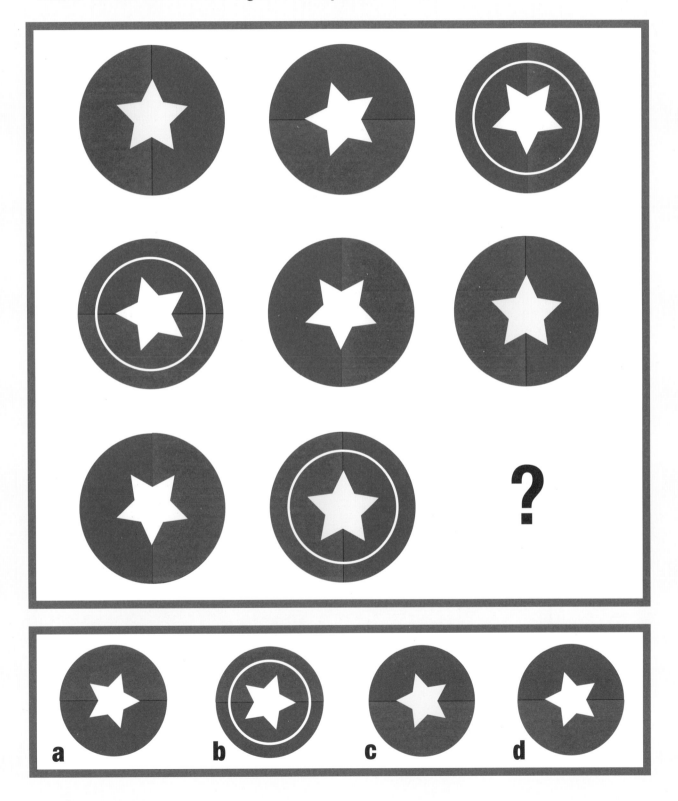

DIFFICULTY ✪✪✪✪✪✪✩✩✩

Target time: 10 minutes

There is only one place in which Pattern a can be found in the grid. The pattern may be rotated but not reflected. Can you find it? Similarly, there are three places in which Pattern b is hidden in the grid. Find them, too.

a

b

10 DIFFICULTY ✪✪✪✪✩✩✩✩✩
Target time: 4 minutes

Cinderella (not pictured here!) has two identical ugly stepsisters. Can you identify them? They might even be reflections of one another, so look carefully.

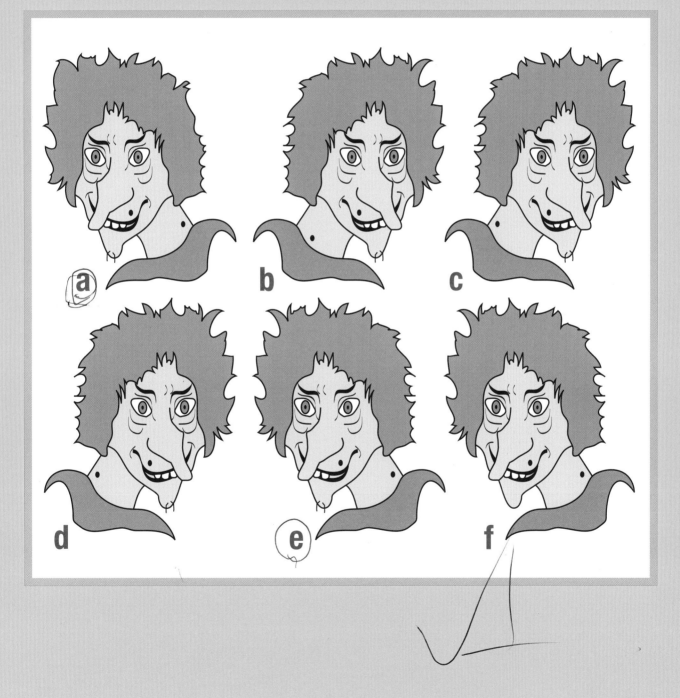

11 DIFFICULTY ✪✪✪✪✪✪✪✪✪

Target time: 4 minutes

When the figure below is folded to form a cube, which one of the following (a, b, c, d, or e) can be reproduced?

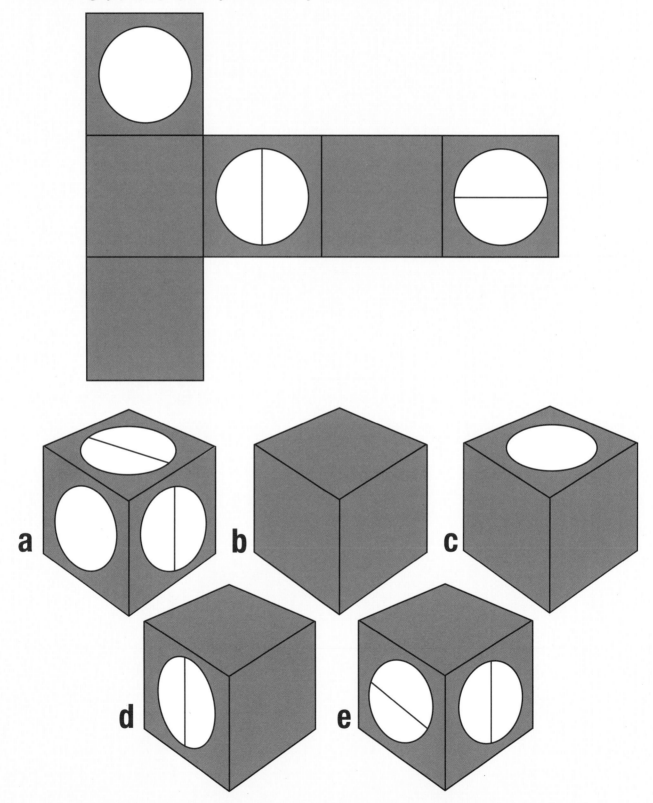

12 DIFFICULTY ✪✪✪✪✪✪✪✪✪✪

Target time: 3 minutes

Which domino (a, b, c, or d) should fill the empty space?

a **b** **c** **d**

13 DIFFICULTY ✪✪✪✪✪✪✪✪✪✪

Target time: 5 minutes

Juliette has lined up these three dice on her coffee table. She can see the same seven faces that you can see. Angelica (her friend, sitting opposite) can see the top three faces of the dice, as well as a further four faces you and Juliette cannot see. None of you can see the bottom three faces of these dice. What is the total number of spots on all the faces of the dice that Angelica can see, given that there aren't six spots visible to anyone on the die furthest right from your point of view as you look at the diagram?

14 DIFFICULTY ✪✪✪✪✪✪✰✰✰✰

Target time: 6 minutes

Should the central circle be a 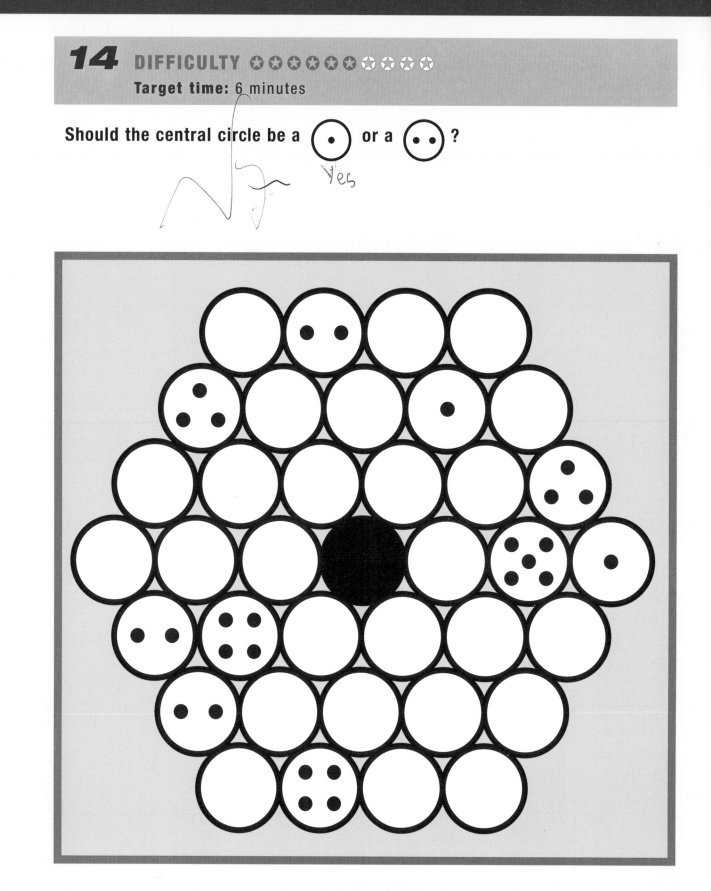 or a ?

15 DIFFICULTY ✪✪✪✪✪✪✪✪✪✪

Target time: 4 minutes

Carefully study the pens below. Which is different from the rest?

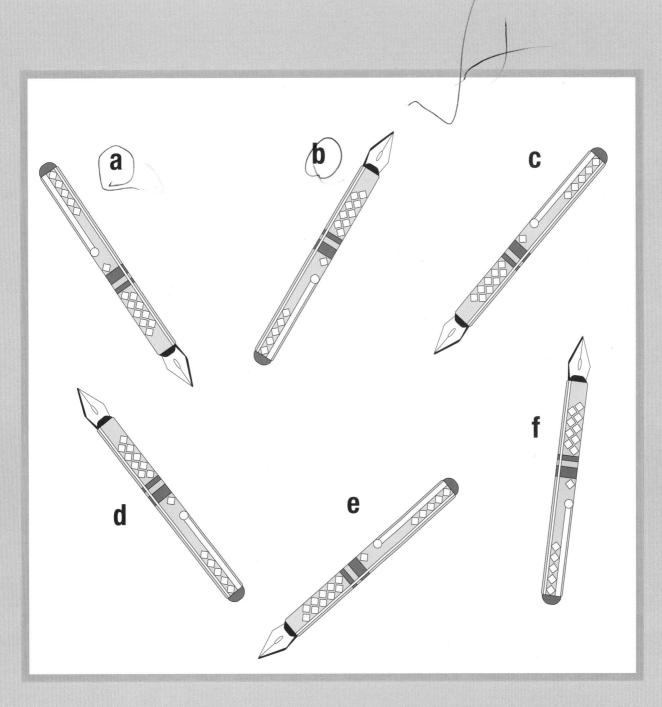

16 DIFFICULTY ✪✪✪✩✩✩✩✩✩✩
Target time: 3 minutes

Color in the shape below. Can you find the minimum number of different colors needed so that no two touching areas are the same color?

17 DIFFICULTY ✪✪✪✩✩✩✩✩✩✩
Target time: 3 minutes

Pat the dog has laid out his bones for your inspection. Can you deduce the order in which he placed them on the pile?

18 DIFFICULTY ✪✪✪✩✩✩✩✩✩✩
Target time: 5 minutes

Get your automobile to the garage, marked with an X, avoiding the potholes as you go.

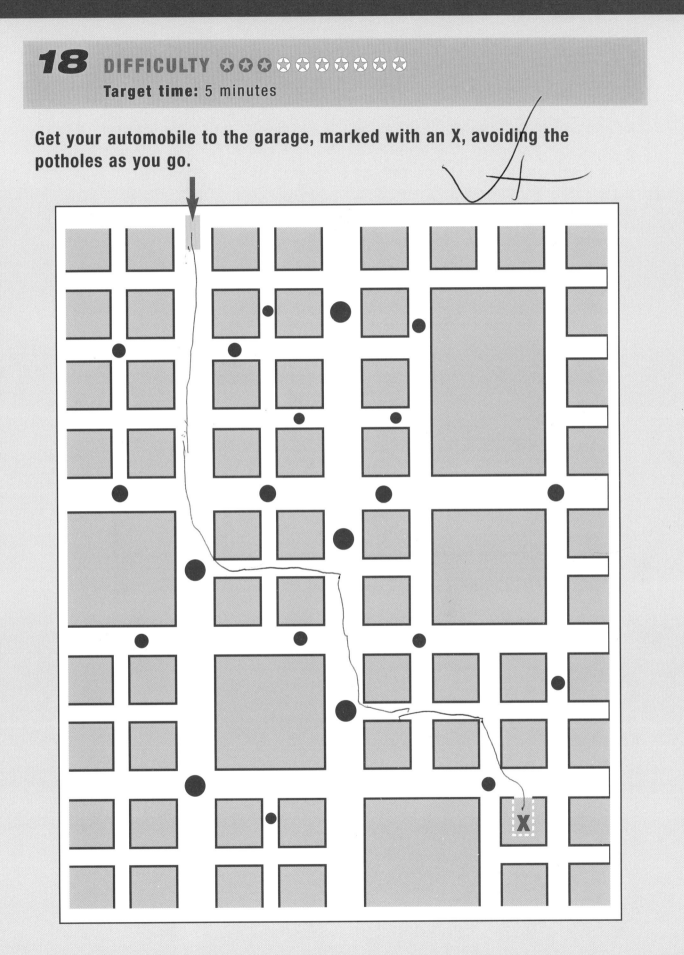

A tangram is an ancient Chinese puzzle. To make your own tangram, take a piece of cardboard (the thicker the better) and draw a 4 x 4 grid pattern on it. Then cut out seven pieces, as indicated by this diagram.

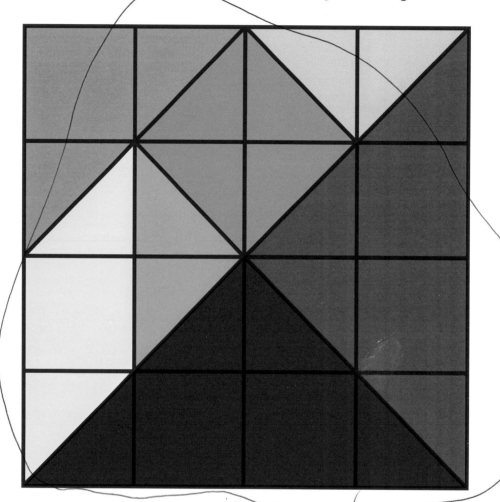

Now rearrange the shapes to make the images on the facing page. You must use all seven pieces each time, and overlapping the pieces is not allowed. We've done one for you, below.

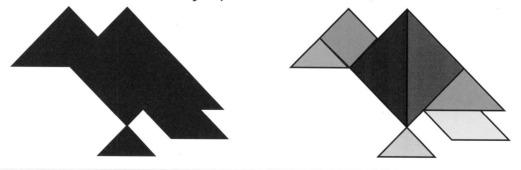

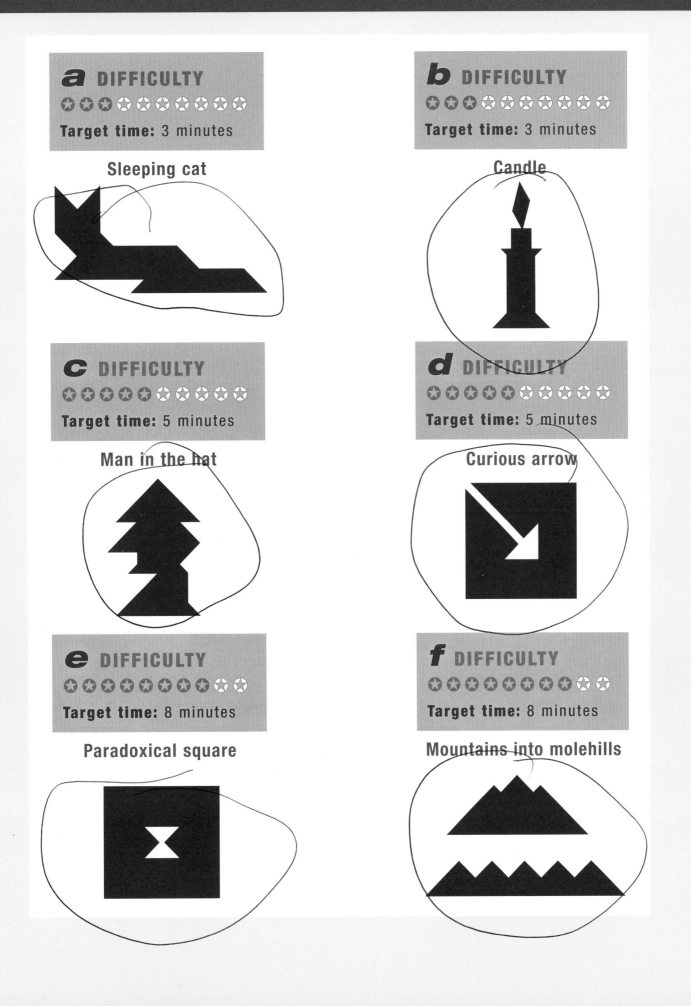

a DIFFICULTY

Target time: 3 minutes

Sleeping cat

b DIFFICULTY

Target time: 3 minutes

Candle

c DIFFICULTY

Target time: 5 minutes

Man in the hat

d DIFFICULTY

Target time: 5 minutes

Curious arrow

e DIFFICULTY

Target time: 8 minutes

Paradoxical square

f DIFFICULTY

Target time: 8 minutes

Mountains into molehills

20 DIFFICULTY ✪✪✪✪✪✪✪✪✪✪
Target time: 8 minutes

When the shape below is folded to form a cube, which one of the following (a, b, c, d, or e) can be produced?

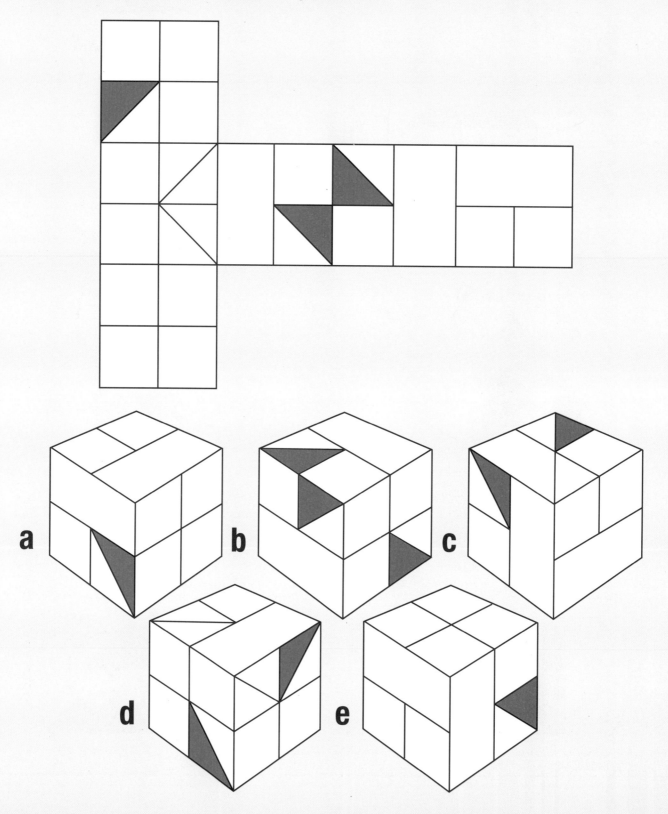

21 DIFFICULTY ✪✪✪✪✪✪✪✪✪✪

Target time: 2 minutes

Which of the four boxed figures at the bottom completes the set above it?

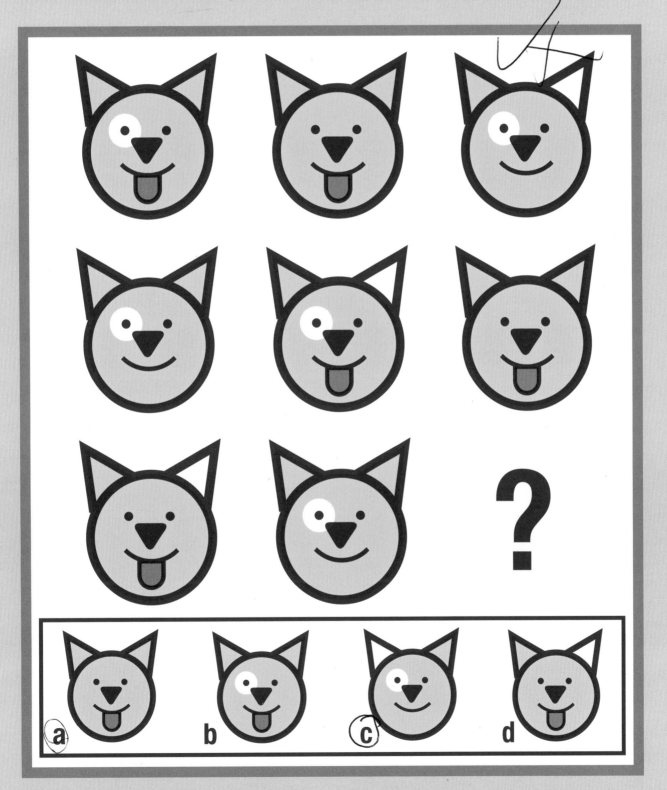

22

DIFFICULTY ✪✪✪✪✪✪✪✪✪✪

Target time: 3 minutes

Which two pieces will fit together perfectly to form a purple copy of this white shape? Pieces may be rotated, but not flipped over.

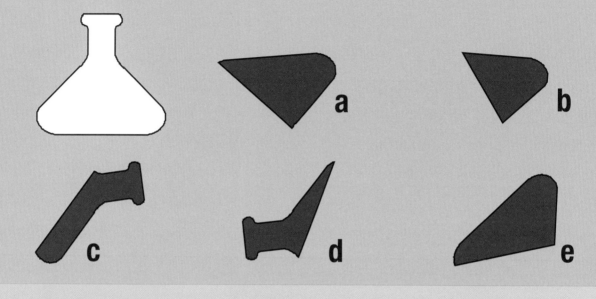

23

DIFFICULTY ✪✪✪✪✪✪✪✪✪✪

Target time: 3 minutes

Which domino (a, b, c, or d) should fill the empty space?

24 DIFFICULTY ✪✪✪✪✩✩✩✩✩

Target time: 5 minutes

Carefully study the pictures below. Which crane is different from the rest?

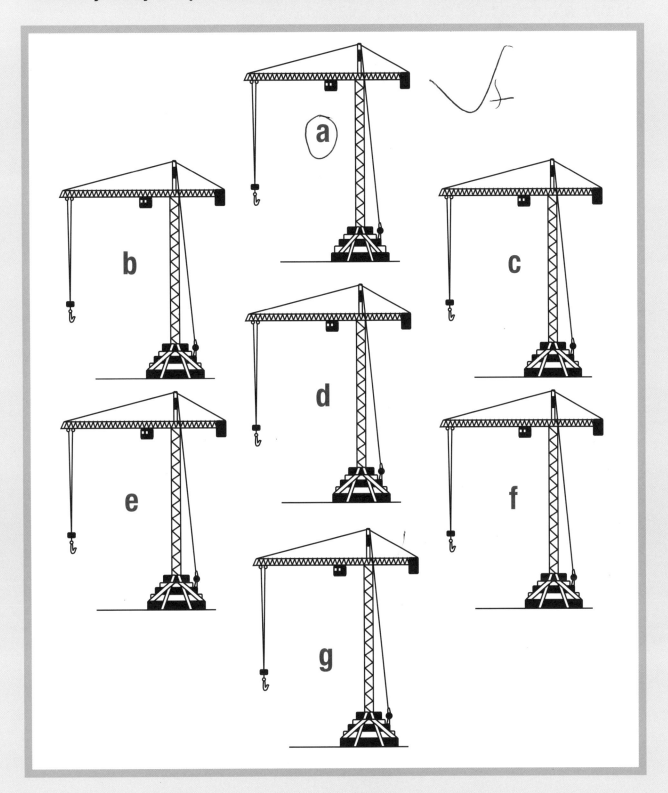

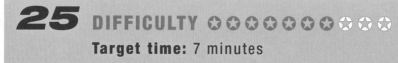

25 DIFFICULTY ✪✪✪✪✪✪✪✪✪

Target time: 7 minutes

What shape should be in the center square? (If you need a clue to help you work out the answer, the colors you see are red, blue, green, yellow, and apricot.)

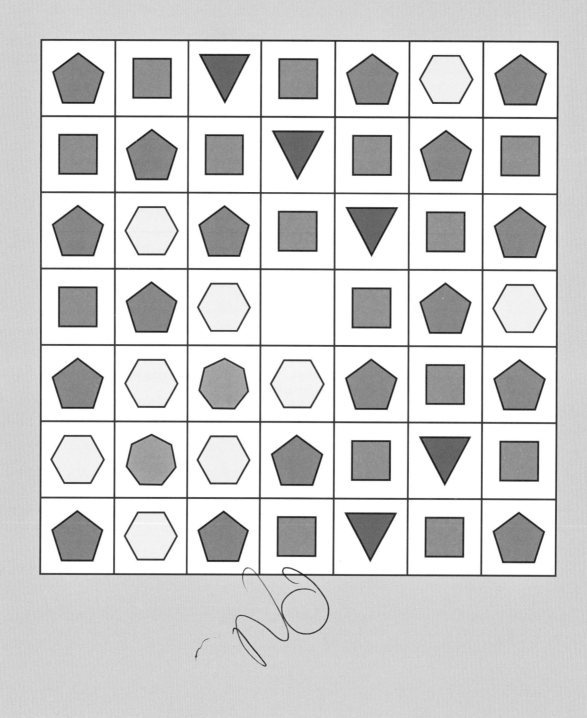

26 DIFFICULTY ✪✪✪✪✪✪✪✪✪✪

Target time: 30 minutes

This nonogram is ripe for solving. (See page 11 for advice on how to complete a nonogram.)

Column clues (read top to bottom, left to right):

Bottom row of column headers:
4, 1, 2, 3, 4, 8, 4, 7, 8, 10, 18, 15, 15, 13, 12, 10, 4, 8, 4, 7, 8, 10, 16, 30, 15, 13, 12, 10, 7, 4

Row above: 3 3 3 4 4 3 3 3 3 · 3 1 2 3 1 7 4 3 3 3 3 3 · 3 2 3 3 2 6

Upper rows (partial): 3 2 4 5 2 1 · 3 · 2 2 3 4 2 2 2 1 · 1 1 2 3 3 3 — 1 — 2 1 3 2 2 2 · 3 2 2 2 — 3 — 2 2 1

Row clues (left side):

	4	1	2	1	1	3
3	2	1	2	2	1	2	1
3	4	2	2	3	1	1	2
3	3	2	2	3	1	1	2
		3	4	8	1	3
			2	4	1	6
		1	4	4	2	1
			5	6	2	2
				8	2	3
			3	6	1	4
		3	6	3	1	3
	2	8	2	2	3
			2	10	3	3
			2	11	4	2
		2	11	2	2	1
				14	4	4
				12	6	3
				12	8	1
				10	3	6
				8	3	6
				4	2	8
					2	10
					2	11
					2	11
						14
						12
						12
						10
						8
						4

27 DIFFICULTY ✪✪✪✪✪✪✪✪✪✪

Target time: 5 minutes

Divide this picture by drawing three straight lines to produce five sections, each containing five different shapes in five different colors.

28 DIFFICULTY ✪✪✪✪✪✪✪✪✪✪

Target time: 5 minutes

What is the minimum number of different colors needed to color in this honeycomb pattern (including the background) in such a way that no two touching areas are the same color?

29 DIFFICULTY ✪✪✪☆☆☆☆☆☆

Target time: 4 minutes

Maggie's magic mirror reflects very strangely! Can you match each vase to its correct (although misplaced and somewhat distorted) image in the mirror on the right?

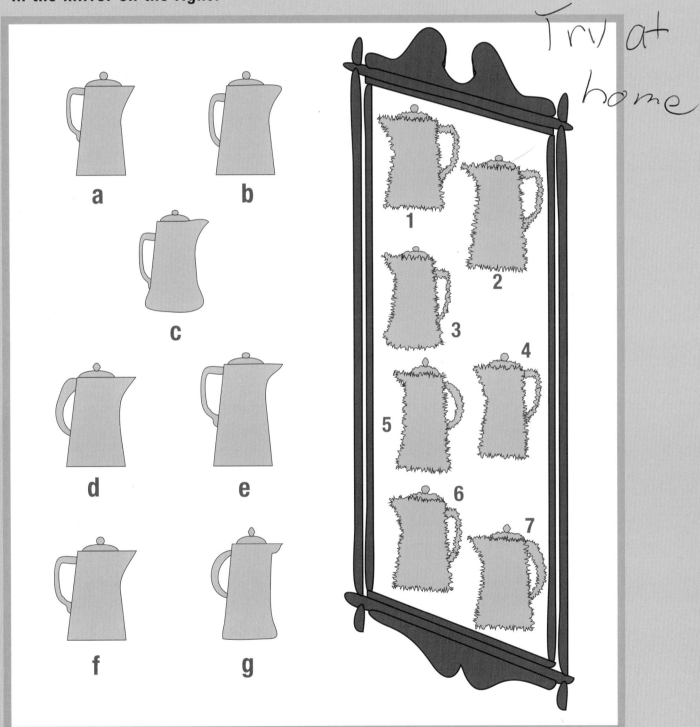

Try at home

30 DIFFICULTY ✮✮✮✮✮✮✮✮✩

Target time: 8 minutes

Dominoes can be arranged into square "picture frames"—this example shows such a frame, where every side adds up to eighteen.

Can you arrange the eight dominoes below into two square frames, each made of four pieces, so that all the sides of both frames add up to nine?

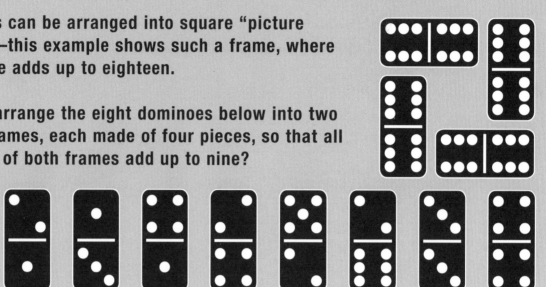

31 DIFFICULTY ✮✮✮✮✮✮✮✩✩✩

Target time: 7 minutes

Divide this picture by drawing two straight lines to produce three sections, each containing two butterflies, four caterpillars, and five larvae.

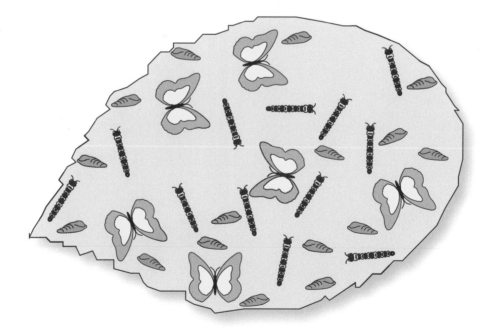

32 DIFFICULTY ✪✪✪✪✪✪✪☆☆☆

Target time: 5 minutes

Study these cupcakes for one minute, then see if you can answer the questions on page 34 without checking back.

[32] DIFFICULTY ✪✪✪✪✪✪✪✩✩✩

Target time: 5 minutes

Can you answer these questions about the puzzle on page 33 without checking back?

1. What color is the frosting on cupcake c? *pink*

2. What color is the case containing cupcake g? *red*

3. How many cupcake cases are blue? *3*

4. How many plates have blue trim? *3*

5. How many of the cherries on cupcake f have a leaf? *1*

6. How many cupcakes are in white cases? *2*

7. How many cupcakes have white frosting? *3*

8. How many cherries does cupcake e have? *4*

33 DIFFICULTY ✪✪✪✪✪✩✩✩✩

Target time: 5 minutes

Can you spot the eight differences between these two pictures? Circle them in the drawing on the right.

Do later

34 DIFFICULTY ✪✪✪✪✪✪✪✪✪✪
Target time: 3 minutes

Which of the four boxed figures at the bottom completes the set?

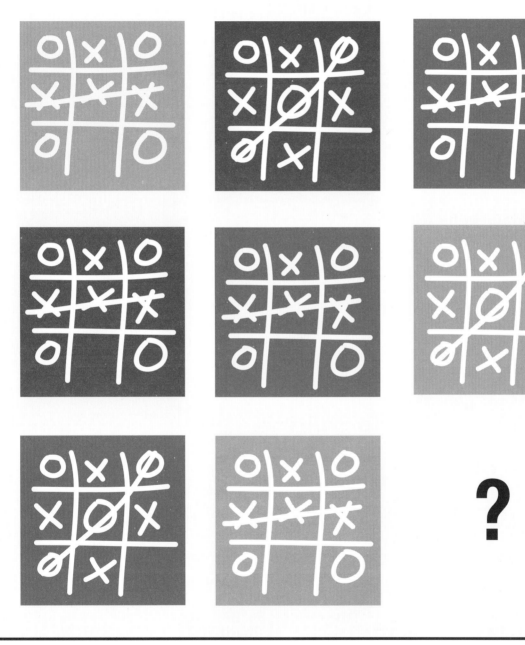

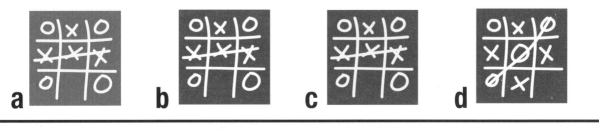

a   b   c   d

35 DIFFICULTY ✪✪✪✪✪✩✩✩✩✩
Target time: 5 minutes

When the shape below is folded to form a cube, which one of the following (a, b, c, d, or e) can be produced?

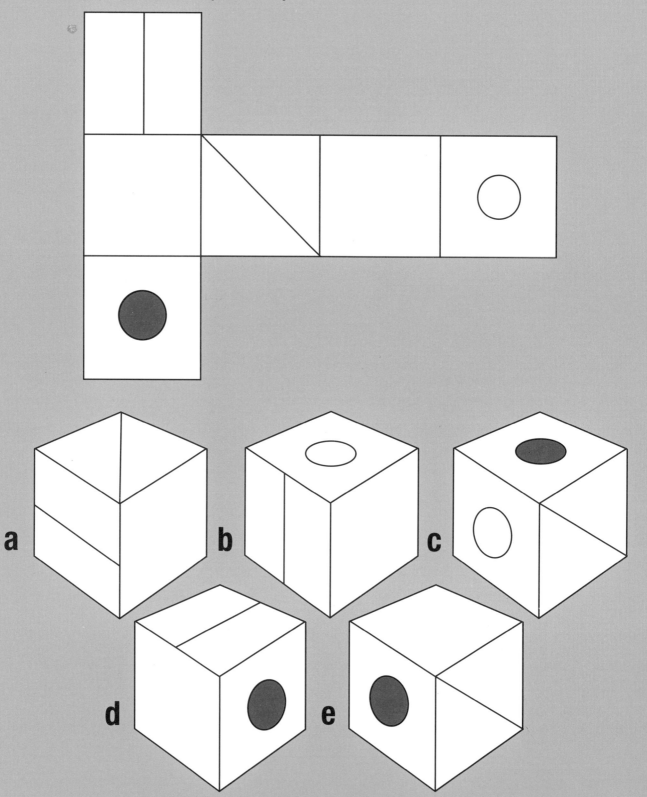

36 DIFFICULTY ✪✪✪✪✪✩✩✩✩✩
Target time: 3 minutes

Which two pieces will fit together perfectly to form a green copy of this white shape? Pieces may be rotated, but not flipped over.

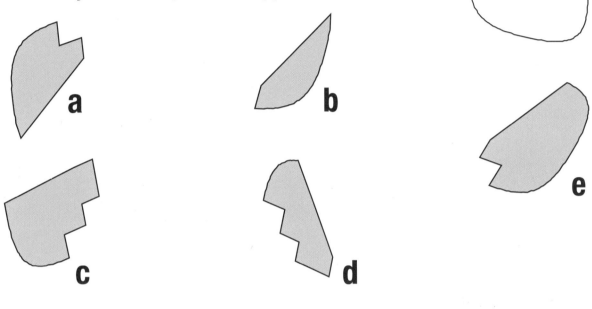

37 DIFFICULTY ✪✪✪✪✩✩✩✩✩✩
Target time: 5 minutes

Starting with the top row of coins, move any two adjacent coins four times, separating the heads from the tails, to end up with the bottom row.

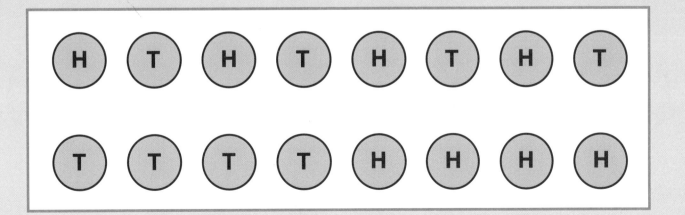

38 DIFFICULTY ✪✪✪✪✪✪✪✪✪✪

Target time: 10 minutes

The square below contains exactly one of each of thirty-six faces from six standard dice. In each horizontal row of six smaller squares, each vertical column of six smaller squares, and both diagonal lines of six smaller squares, there are faces with different numbers of spots.

We've placed a few to give you a start, but can you provide the rest using only the given clues?

1. The face of the die in square 3 has the same number of spots as that in square 32.
2. The face of the die in square 14 has the same number of spots as that in square 31.
3. The face of the die in square 25 has the same number of spots as that in square 36.

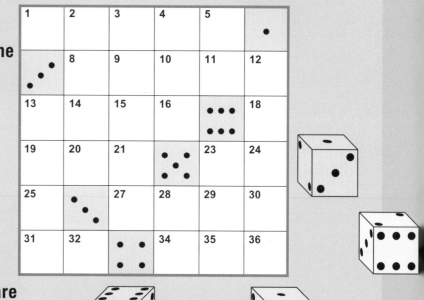

39 DIFFICULTY ✪✪✪✪✪✪✪✪✪✪

Target time: 5 minutes

Here are five clocks. Four are perfect, but the fifth was damaged. Can you determine the time on clock e?

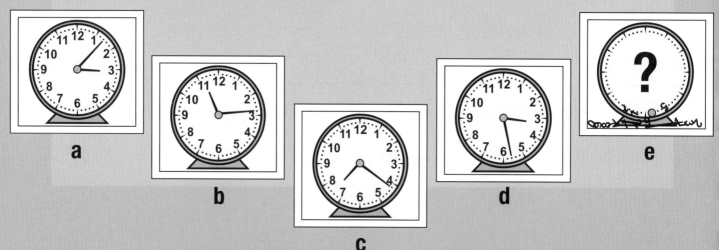

40 DIFFICULTY ✪✪✪✪✪✪✪✪✪✪

Target time: 7 minutes

Carefully study the diagrams below. Which is different from the rest?

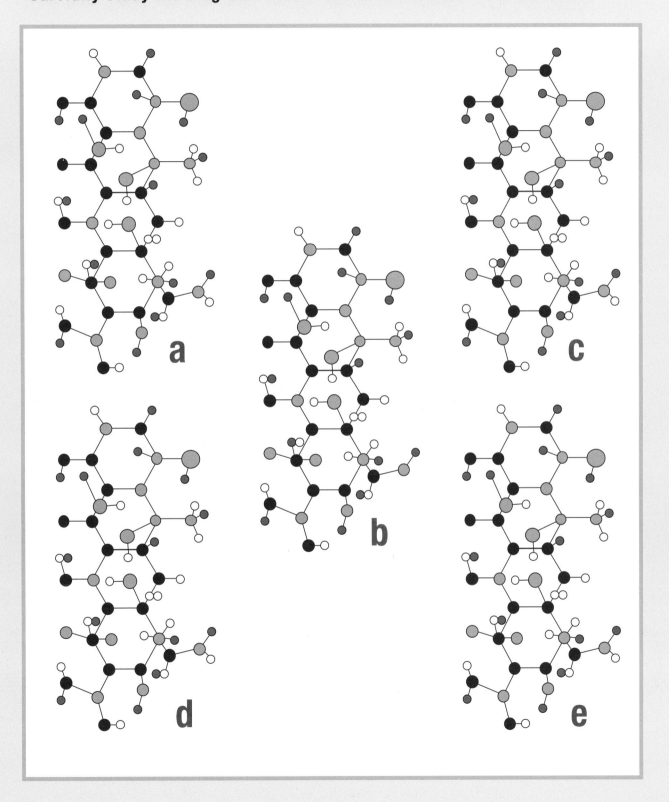

41 DIFFICULTY ✪✪✪✪✪☆☆☆☆☆

Target time: 6 minutes

Find your way through the woods from the cabin at the top to the picnic table marked with an X.

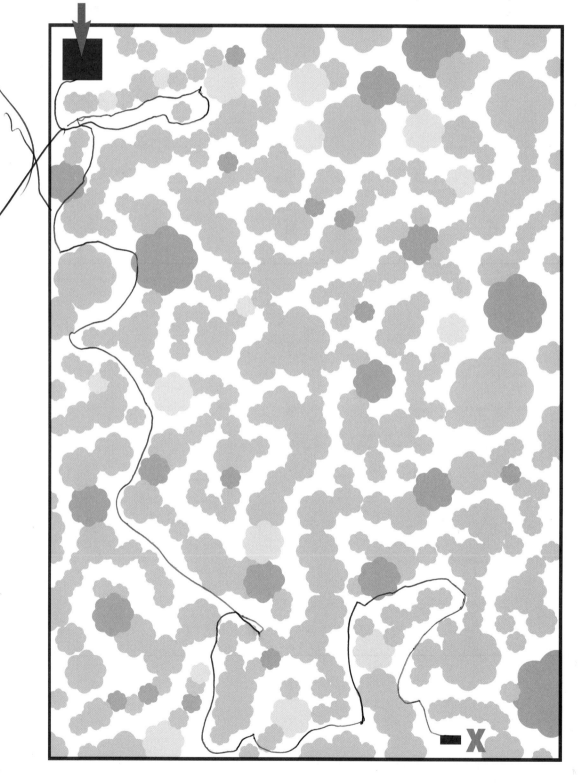

42 DIFFICULTY ✪✪✪✪✪✪✪✪✪✪

Target time: 6 minutes

Find a route from the top to the bottom down through the pipes, avoiding any blockages.

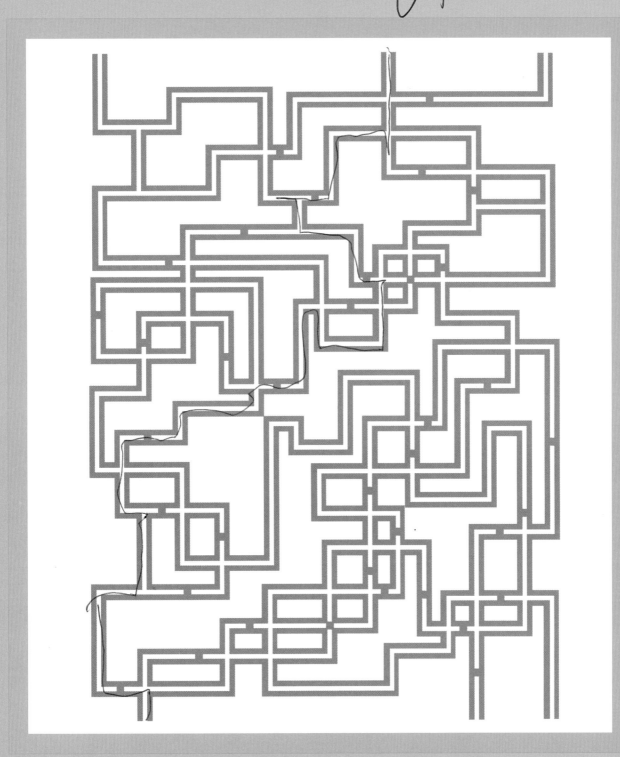

43 DIFFICULTY ✪✪✪✪✪✪✪✪✪✪

Target time: 5 minutes

Can you deduce the minimum number of different colors needed to color in the diagram in such a way that no two touching areas are the same?

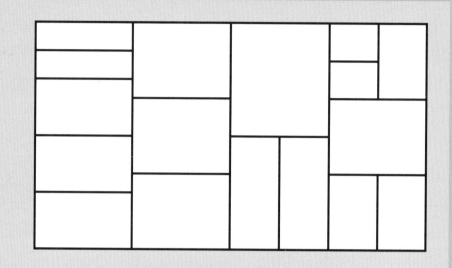

44 DIFFICULTY ✪✪✪✪✪✪✪✪✪✪

Target time: 10 minutes

The square below contains one of each of thirty-six faces from six standard dice. In each horizontal row of six smaller squares and each vertical column of six smaller squares, there are faces with different numbers of spots. Also in the long diagonal line of six smaller squares from top left to bottom right, there are faces with different numbers of spots. In the long diagonal line from top right to bottom left, however, no face has four spots, but there are faces with five different numbers. We've placed a few to give you a start. Given that the total number of spots on the four corner dice equals fourteen, can you place the rest?

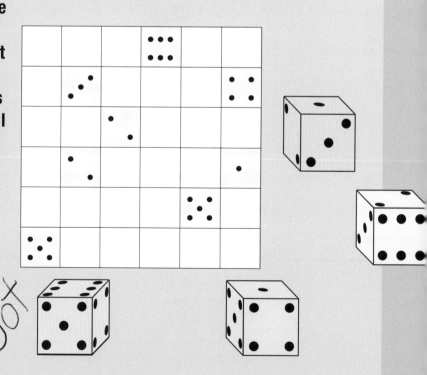

45 DIFFICULTY ✪✪✪✪✪✪✪✪✪✪

Target time: 12 minutes

1. There is only one place in which Pattern a can be found in the grid. The pattern may be rotated but not reflected. Can you find it?
2. Similarly, there are six places in which Pattern b is hidden in the grid. Can you find them?

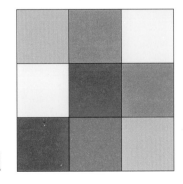

a

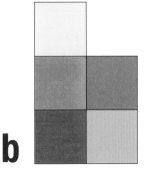

b

Not

46 DIFFICULTY ✪✪✪☆☆☆☆☆☆☆

Target time: 3 minutes

Can you spot the six differences between these two pictures?
Circle them in the drawing on the right.

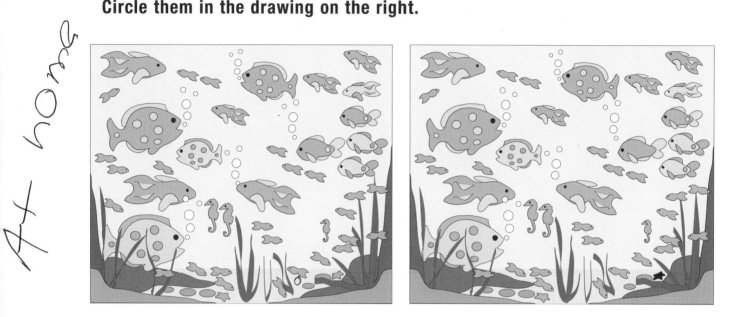

47 DIFFICULTY ✪✪✪✪✪☆☆☆☆

Target time: 6 minutes

Can you divide
this square on
the right into
four identical
shapes, each
composed of
sixteen smaller
squares, and
each containing
four different
shapes?

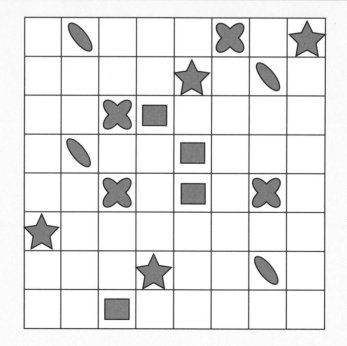

48 DIFFICULTY ✪✪✪✪✪✩✩✩✩✩
Target time: 3 minutes

Which two pieces will fit together perfectly to form a red copy of this white star? Pieces may be rotated, but not flipped over.

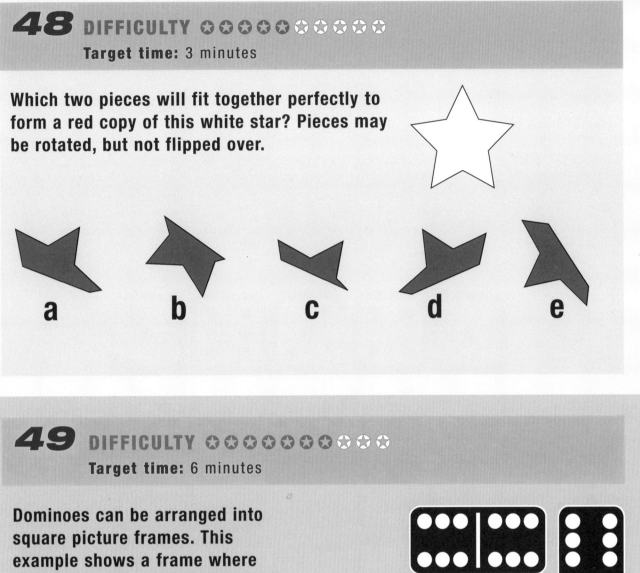

a   **b**   **c**   **d**   **e**

49 DIFFICULTY ✪✩✩✩✩✩✩✩✩✩
Target time: 6 minutes

Dominoes can be arranged into square picture frames. This example shows a frame where every side adds up to eighteen. Can you arrange the eight dominoes below into two square frames made of four pieces each, so that all the sides of both frames add up to ten?

50 DIFFICULTY ✪✪✪✪✪✪✪✪✪✪

Target time: 6 minutes

Slide one of the dominoes marked by an arrow into the center to complete the hidden pattern. Which one of the four should it be?

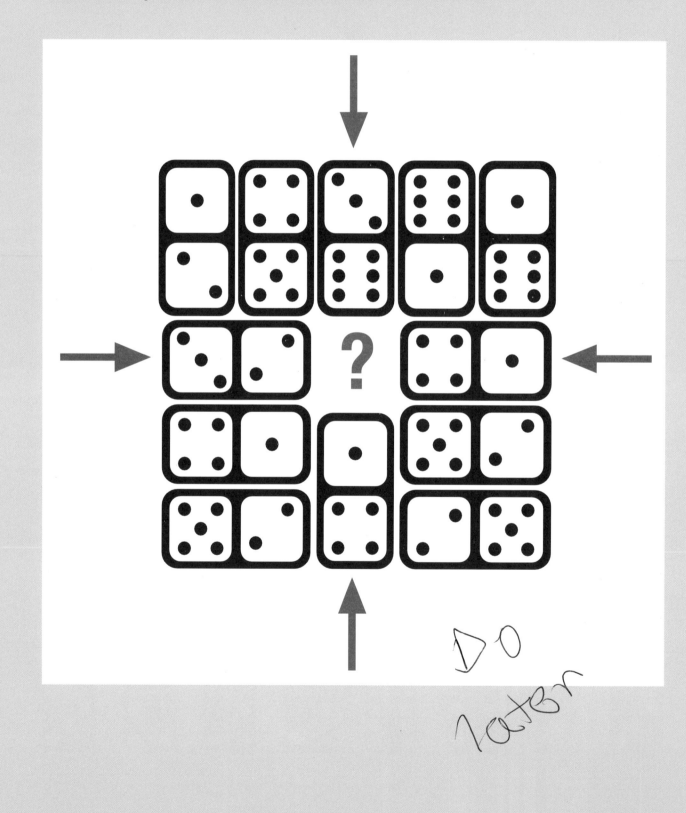

51 DIFFICULTY ✪✪✪✪✪✪☆☆☆

Target time: 7 minutes

Only two of these vases of flowers are the same. Can you identify them? They might even be reflections of one another, so look closely!

At home

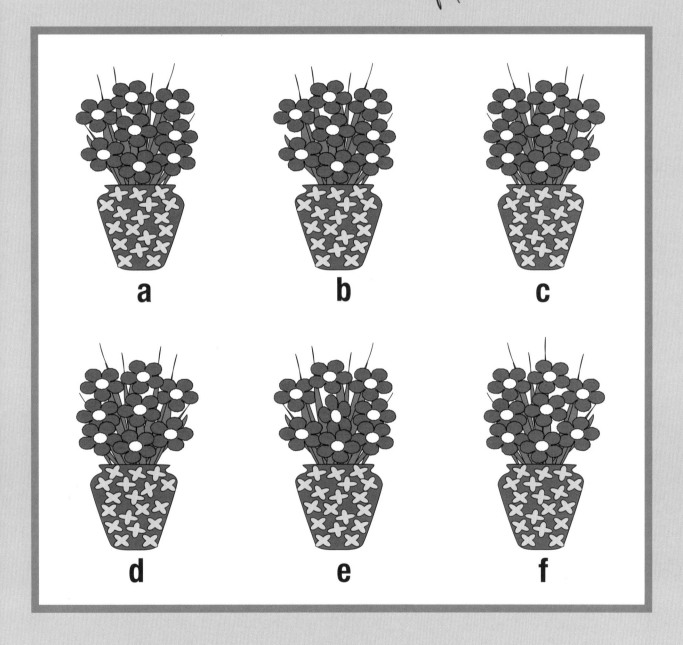

52 DIFFICULTY ✪✪✪✪✪✪✪✪✪✪

Target time: 15 minutes

This is a one-player solitaire game. Place four silver coins on spaces 1 to 4, and four pennies on spaces 5 to 8. The aim is to make the coins swap sides by sliding them from circle to circle. Only one coin per space is allowed, and coins must not jump one another.

How many moves are there in the shortest solution? One move counts as sliding one coin from one space to another in a straight line, moving through any number of unoccupied spaces along the way.

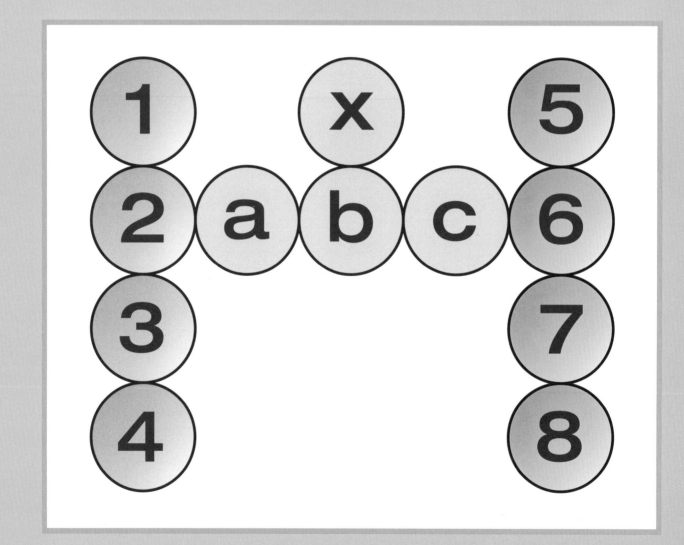

53 DIFFICULTY ✪✪✪✪✪✪✪✪✪✪

Target time: 30 minutes

Don't be scared by this nonogram! (See page 11 for advice on how to complete a nonogram.)

Column clues (top):

							1																								
					1	1	3																								
					1	3	1																								
				4	2	2	4					1			1															
	4	3	2	2	4	5	4	2	6			1		2	1		1													
	1	2	2	3	2	1	1	3	2		6		2	1	2	1	1	2	2	2	2	4	4	5	7	12				
10	6	5	4	5	4	3	1	2	3	1	7	7	19	12	4	9	2	8	4	2	1	4	3	1	2	1	1	1	1	
11	9	10	2	2	2	1	1	1	1	1	1	16	1	1	12	1	13	1	1	2	1	1	1	2	2	2	3	7	11	

Row clues (left):

				11	11
				8	8
		5	3	5	
	4	1	2	5	
		3	4	3	
	2	5	2	2	
		1	8	2	
		1	5	1	
		1	6	1	
		1	7	1	
		2	3	1	
		1	1	1	
				7	
				12	
			8	3	
	4	7	2	5	
		5	8	4	
			6	13	
			6	10	
		1	10	1	
		1	17	1	
		8	8	1	
		7	9	1	
		6	9	2	
3	1	3	1	1	2
	3	3	1	1	2
		3	2	2	2
3	1	3	3	3	
			6	6	
			11	9	

54 DIFFICULTY ✪✪✪✪✪✪☆☆☆☆
Target time: 6 minutes

In the sequence below, which of the lettered alternatives (a, b, c, or d) should replace the question mark?

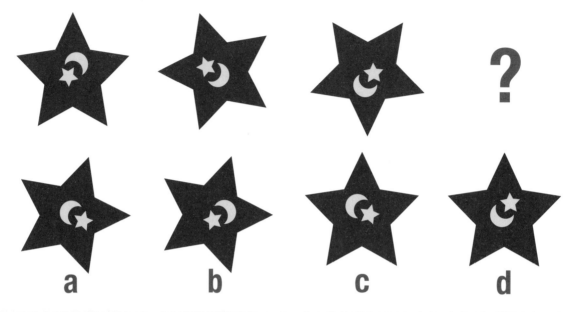

a   **b**   **c**   **d**

55 DIFFICULTY ✪☆✪✪✪✪☆☆☆☆
Target time: 6 minutes

Can you spot the eight differences between these two pictures? Circle them in the drawing on the right.

56 DIFFICULTY ✪✪✪✪✪✪✪✪✪✪

Target time: 2 minutes

Which domino (a, b, c, or d) should fill the empty space?

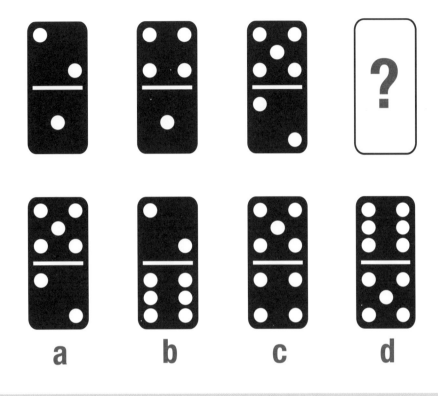

a   b   c   d

57 DIFFICULTY ✪✪✪✪✪✪✪✪✪✪

Target time: 5 minutes

You may well need a break after deciding which two pieces fit together perfectly to form a mirror image copy of this teacup. Pieces may be rotated, but not flipped over.

a   b   c   d   e

58 DIFFICULTY ✪✪✪✪✪✪☆☆✪

Target time: 7 minutes

At first glance, these diggers may look the same, but only two are identical. They might even be reflections of one another. How quickly can you decide which two are the same?

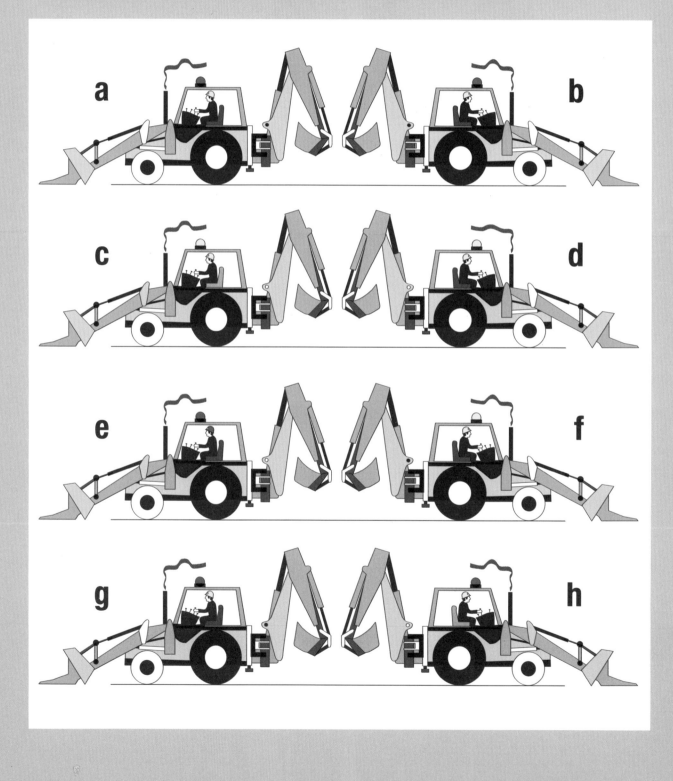

59 DIFFICULTY ✪✪✪✪✪✰✰✰✰✰
Target time: 4 minutes

Which of the four boxed figures (a, b, c, or d) completes the set?

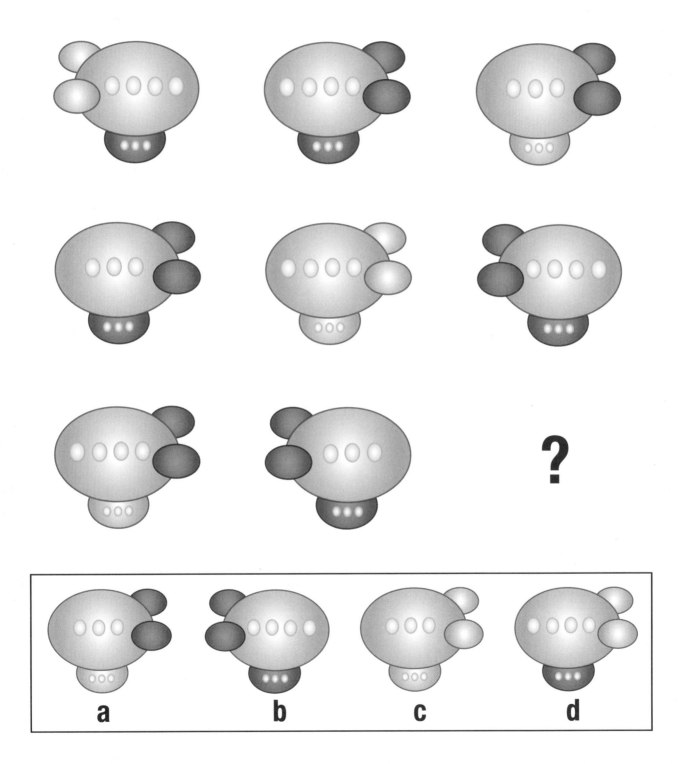

60 DIFFICULTY ✪✪✪✪✪✪✩✩✩✩

Target time: 5 minutes

Change all the rows either to all heads or all tails, without touching more than ONE coin.

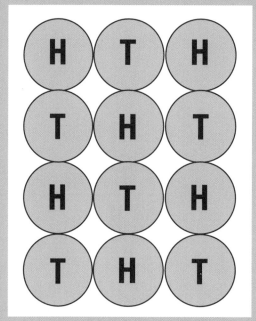

61 DIFFICULTY ✪✪✪✪✪✪✪✩✩✩

Target time: 7 minutes

Can you divide this square into four identical shapes, each composed of sixteen squares, and each containing five different chess pieces?

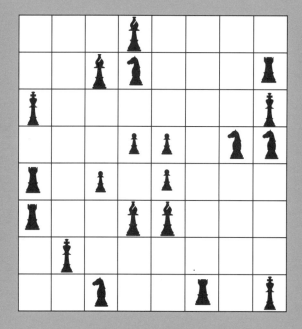

62 DIFFICULTY ✪✪✪✪✪✪✪✪✪✪

Target time: 8 minutes

Can you make a whole plate, identical to the one shown, from any of these pieces? If so, which ones? Pieces may be rotated, but not flipped over.

a   b   c

d   e   f

g   h   i

63 DIFFICULTY ✪✪✪✪✪✪✩✩✩✩

Target time: 3 minutes

If ⌒ ⌒ is to ⌒ ⌒

then ⌒ ⌒ is to:

a

b

c

d

e

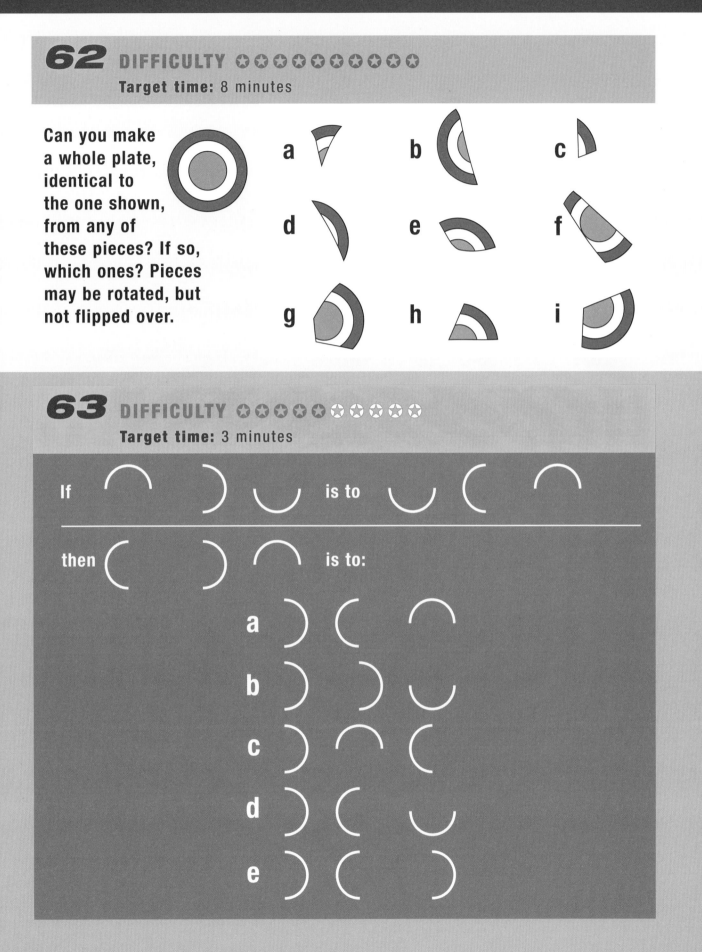

64 DIFFICULTY ✪✪✪✪✪✪✪✪✪✪
Target time: 6 minutes

Find your way through the maze. X marks the exit.

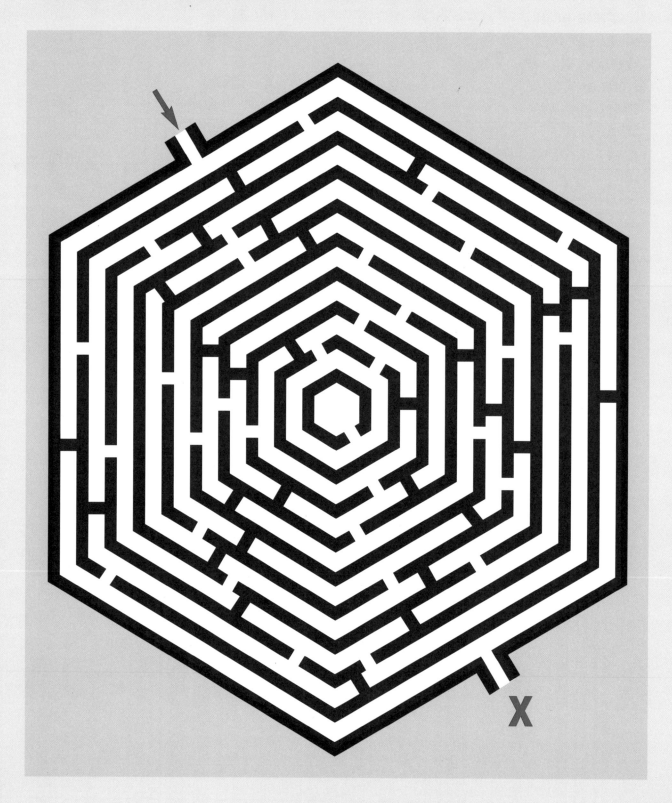

65 DIFFICULTY ✪✪✪✪✪✪✪✪☆☆

Target time: 6 minutes

Study these nine sets of chairs, lamps, and tables for one minute, then see if you can answer the questions on page 58.

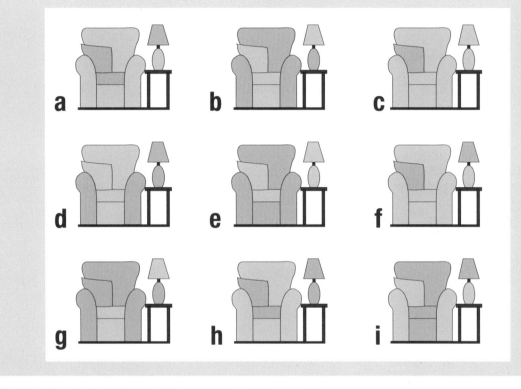

66 DIFFICULTY ✪✪✪✪✪☆☆☆☆☆

Target time: 5 minutes

Can you spot the eight differences between these two pictures? Circle them in the picture on the right.

[65] DIFFICULTY ✪✪✪✪✪✪✪☆☆
Target time: 6 minutes

Can you answer these questions about the puzzle on page 57 without checking back?

1. What color is the cushion on chair f?

2. What color are the arms of chair g?

3. How many lamps have both an orange shade and an orange base?

4. How many chairs have both a green cushion and a green seat?

5. How many chairs have both an orange back and a green seat?

6. How many lamps have both a green shade and a green base?

7. How many lamps have both an orange shade and a green base?

8. What color is the shade on the lamp next to chair h?

67 DIFFICULTY ✪✪✪✪✪✪✪✪☆
Target time: 8 minutes

Ten dominoes have been used to build this wall, but seven have been masked out. Can you place the missing dominoes in the correct places, bearing in mind that each vertical line of four numbers (as well as the two end vertical lines of two numbers) adds up to ten; the second horizontal row of dominoes has dots totaling sixteen, and the third horizontal row of dominoes has dots totaling ten?

68 DIFFICULTY ✪✪✪✪✩✩✩✩✩✩

Target time: 4 minutes

Carefully study the clowns below. Which one is different from the rest?

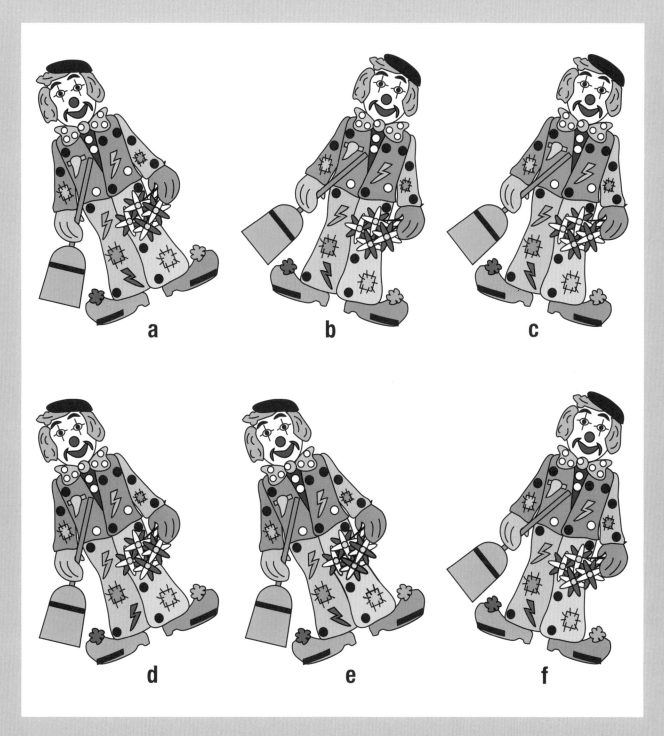

a   b   c

d   e   f

69 DIFFICULTY ✪✪✪✪☆☆☆☆☆☆
Target time: 4 minutes

When the shape below is folded to form a cube, which one of the following (a, b, c, d, or e) is produced?

70 DIFFICULTY ✪✪✪✪✪✪✰✰✰✰

Target time: 6 minutes

Place the pieces from a standard set of twenty-eight dominoes into the following grid by matching their numbers with those in the rectangle. It's trickier than you might think, so we've placed one in position and supplied a checklist, which may help!

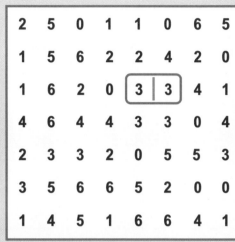

2	5	0	1	1	0	6	5
1	5	6	2	2	4	2	0
1	6	2	0	3	3	4	1
4	6	4	4	3	3	0	4
2	3	3	2	0	5	5	3
3	5	6	6	5	2	0	0
1	4	5	1	6	6	4	1

71 DIFFICULTY ✪✪✪✪✪✰✰✰✰✰

Target time: 4 minutes

Match the arrow flights with the correct arrowheads. If you pick the correct five, a name will be spelled out.

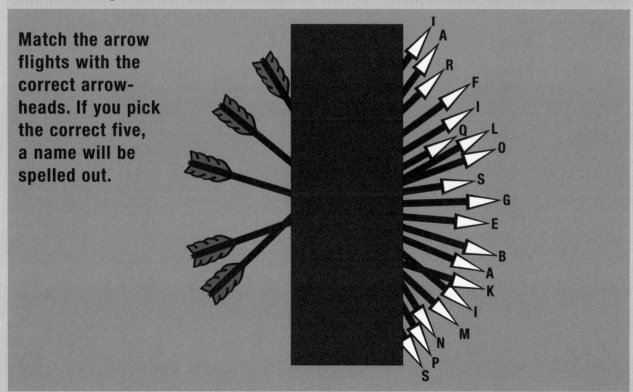

72 DIFFICULTY ✪✪✪✪✪✪✪☆☆☆
Target time: 7 minutes

At first glance, these dresses may look the same, but only two are identical. Can you determine which two?

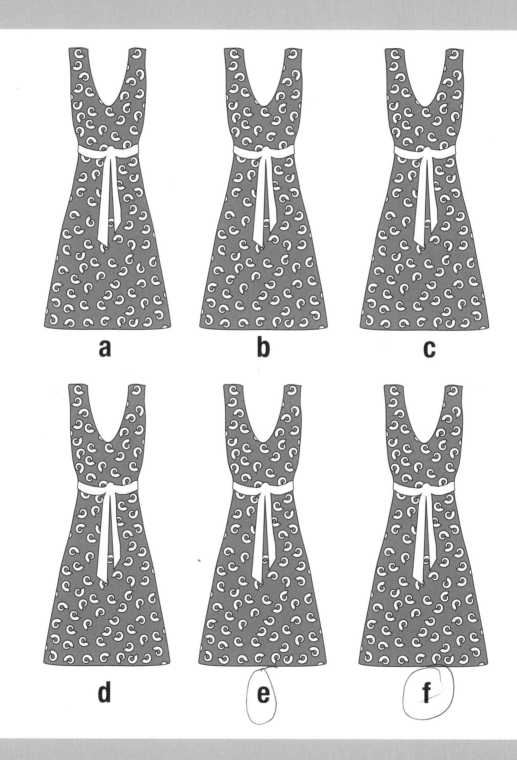

a   b   c

d   e   f

73

DIFFICULTY ✪✪✪✩✩✩✩✩✩✩

Target time: 2 minutes

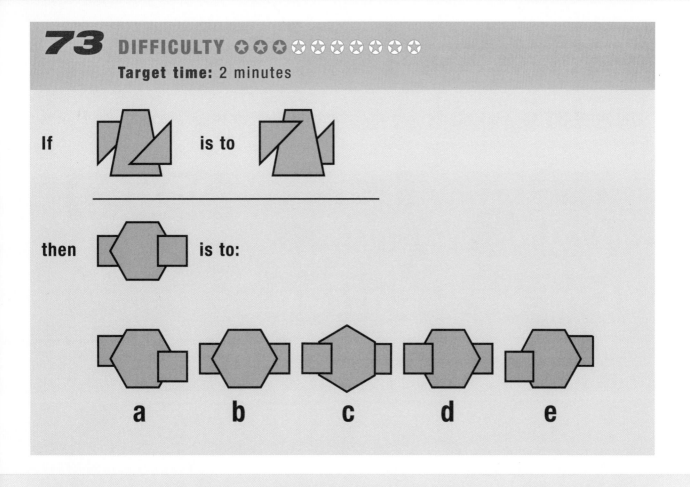

If [shape] is to [shape]

then [shape] is to:

a   b   c   d   e

74

DIFFICULTY ✪✩✩✩✩✩✩✩✩✩

Target time: 5 minutes

Can you color in this simplified version of a map of the U.S. so that no two touching areas are the same, using just four colors? You may use colored pens.

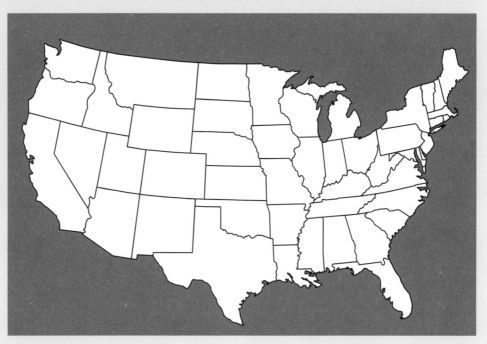

75 DIFFICULTY ✪✪✪✪✪☆☆☆☆
Target time: 4 minutes

Which of the four boxed figures (a, b, c, or d) completes the set?

76 DIFFICULTY ✪✪✪✪✪✪✪✪✪✪

Target time: 30 minutes

A little bird has told us that this nonogram is waiting to be solved. (See page 11 for advice on how to complete a nonogram.)

Column clues (top):

						2		3																					
			2	2	1	2	4	4		15																			
			2	3	1	2	2	7	14	1	11	11	11							3	3	2							
1	2	2	2	6	3	2	2	2	3	2	3	2	1	12	12			6	4	2	2	2	1						
22	17	12	9	5	4	4	5	2	3	4	2	2	2	3	2	1	13	13	14	7	8	5	2	2	1	1	2	2	1

Row clues (left):

				5
				7
			1	4
	4	1	3	
			3	2
			1	2
			1	4
			1	8
			1	11
		1	2	9
		1	1	10
		1	1	10
		1	1	11
		2	1	11
		2	2	12
		2	1	13
		2	2	14
		2	2	13
	3	2	6	3
		3	12	6
3	2	2	5	3
	4	2	2	6
	4	2	2	8
4	2	2	3	4
		15	3	
		13	4	
		8	3	
		6	3	
		5	4	
	4	1	1	

77 DIFFICULTY ✪✪✪✪✪✪✪✩✩✩
Target time: 5 minutes

Peter enjoys selling his wares at the local market on Saturdays. One day he decided to play a little game with his regular customers. Five customers agreed to play and each threw two dice. Their throws and rewards are shown on the right—except Mary's, where you can see only the dice she threw. Can you determine exactly how Peter determined how many loaves and fish each customer should get, and precisely what quantity of loaves and fish he awarded to Mary?

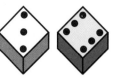

Andrew
= 8 loaves
and 2 fish

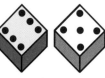

John
= 4 loaves
and 2 fish

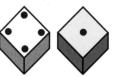

Elizabeth
= 6 loaves
and 12 fish

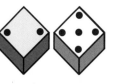

James
= 8 loaves
and 6 fish

Mary
= ? loaves
and ? fish

78 DIFFICULTY ✪✪✪✪✪✪✪✩✩✩
Target time: 5 minutes

Can you spot the eight differences between these two pictures? Circle them in the drawing on the right.

79 DIFFICULTY ✪✪✪✪✪✪✪☆☆☆
Target time: 5 minutes

A table has been set for a children's party. Study the seating plan for one minute, then see if you can answer the questions on page 68 without checking back.

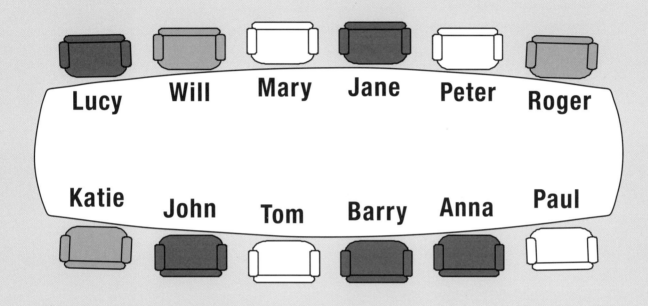

80 DIFFICULTY ✪✪✪✪✪✪✪☆☆☆
Target time: 5 minutes

Study these vases of flowers for one minute, then see if you can answer the questions on page 68 without checking back.

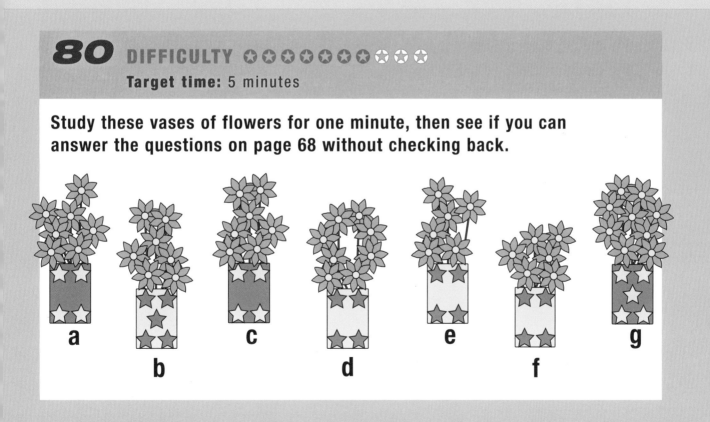

[79] DIFFICULTY ✪✪✪✪✪✪✪✪✪✪

Target time: 5 minutes

Can you answer these questions about the puzzle on page 67 (top) without checking back?

1. Who will sit between Tom and Anna?

2. Who will sit directly opposite Paul?

3. Which boy has the shortest name?

4. What color is Mary's seat?

5. How many chairs are red?

6. How many chairs are white?

7. How many children have names ending in a, e, i, o, or u?

8. How many children will sit directly between (and on the same side of the table as) Lucy and Peter?

[80] DIFFICULTY ✪✪✪✪✪✪✪✪✪✪

Target time: 5 minutes

Can you answer these questions about the puzzle on page 67 (bottom) without checking back?

1. Which two vases have six flowers each?

2. Which vase has the greatest number of flowers?

3. How many vases are green with yellow stars?

4. How many green vases have five yellow stars?

5. How many yellow vases hold seven flowers?

6. How many petals does each flower have?

7. How many vases have eight flowers each?

8. What is the total number of stars on all of the vases combined?

81 DIFFICULTY ✪✪✪✪✪✪✪✪✪
Target time: 8 minutes

Find a route from left to right through the maze.

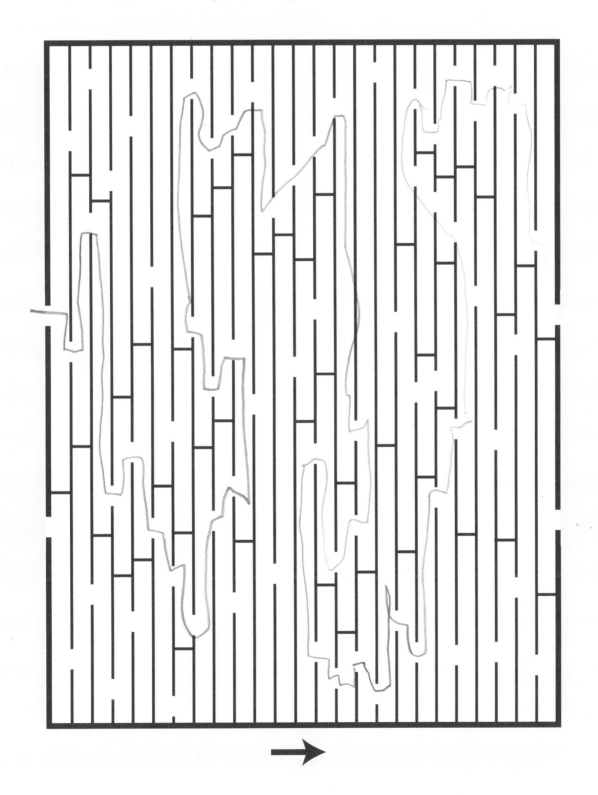

82 DIFFICULTY ✪✪✪✪✪✪✪✪✪✪

Target time: 12 minutes

How many times can you find Pattern a in the hexagonal grid? The pattern may be rotated but not reflected. Pattern b can be found in only one place in the grid. Can you find it?

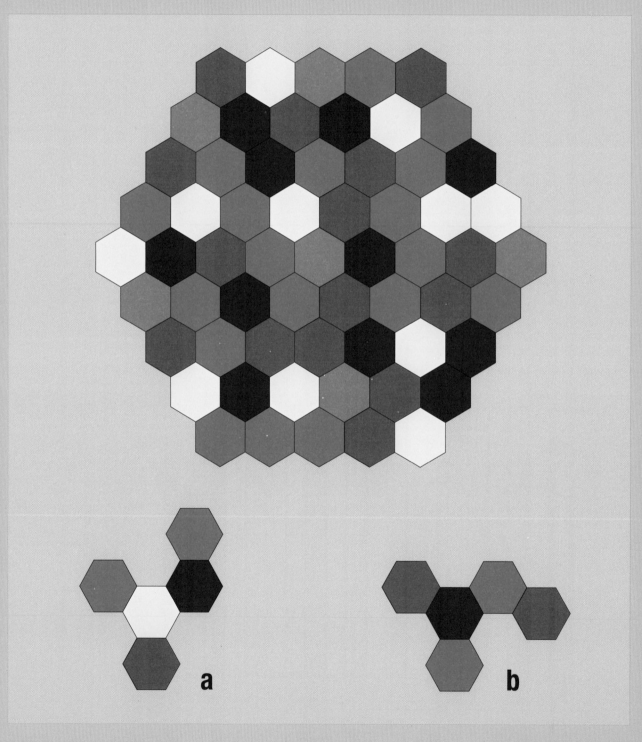

a

b

83 DIFFICULTY ✪✪✪✪✪✪✪✩✩✩
Target time: 7 minutes

One of these piles of mail differs in some way from the others—which is it?

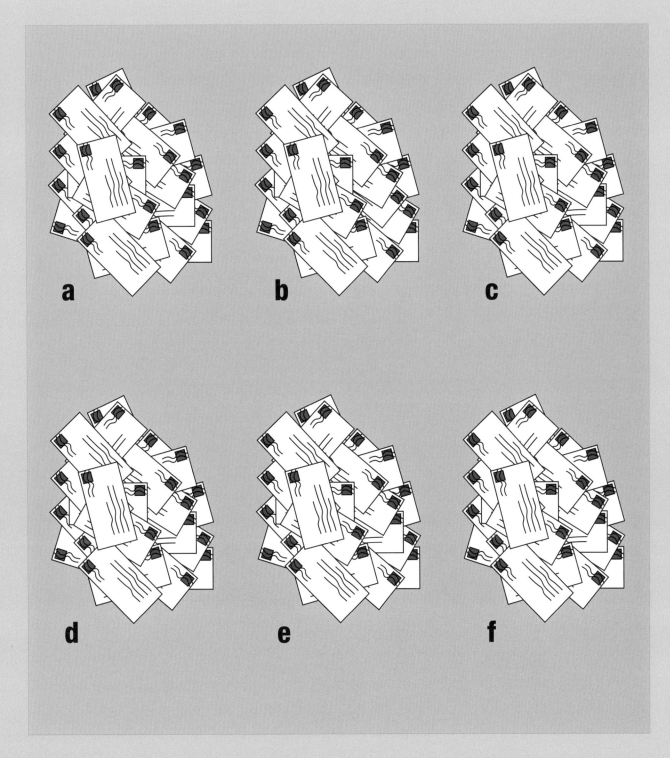

84 DIFFICULTY ✪✪✪✪✪✪✪✪☆☆

Target time: 30 minutes

Aren't you just burning with curiosity to find the solution to this nonogram? (See page 11 for advice on how to complete a nonogram.)

85 DIFFICULTY ✪✪✪✪✪✪☆☆☆☆

Target time: 5 minutes

When the shape below is folded to form a cube, which one of the following (a, b, c, d, or e) is produced?

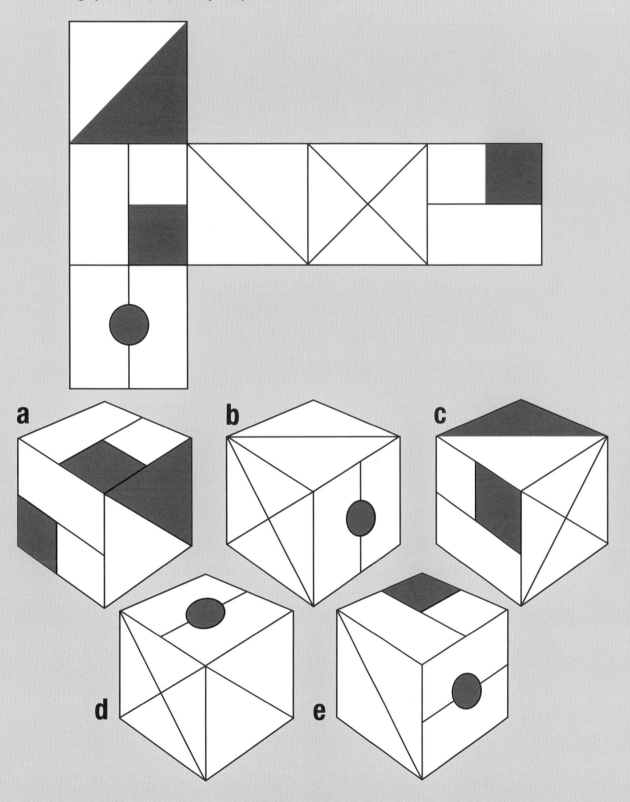

86 DIFFICULTY ✪✪✪✪✪✪✪✪☆☆

Target time: 7 minutes

Florence played a game of Snakes and Ladders with her brother Tom. He threw the first 6, so he started first, placing his playing piece on square 6. After that, every time it was Florence's turn, her die followed the sequence 6, 5, 4, 3, 2, 1; so her first move was to square 6, then to square 11, etc. After his first turn when he threw the 6, Tom's die followed the sequence 1, 2, 3, 4, 5, 6 each time, so his second move was to square 7, his third was to 9, etc. The normal rules of the game were followed, so whenever someone landed on a square that had the foot of a ladder, the piece was moved to the top of the ladder. Whenever someone landed on a square that had the head of a snake, the piece was moved to the tail of the snake. The number thrown to end the game didn't necessarily matter, since the first person to move a piece completely off the board won. Who won the game—Florence or Tom?

FINISH									
100	99	98	97	96	95	94	93	92	91
81	82	83	84	85	86	87	88	89	90
80	79	78	77	76	75	74	73	72	71
61	62	63	64	65	66	67	68	69	70
60	59	58	57	56	55	54	53	52	51
41	42	43	44	45	46	47	48	49	50
40	39	38	37	36	35	34	33	32	31
21	22	23	24	25	26	27	28	29	30
20	19	18	17	16	15	14	13	12	11
1	2	3	4	5	6	7	8	9	10

START

87 DIFFICULTY ✪✪✪✪✪✪✪✪✪✪
Target time: 6 minutes

What color should be in the central triangle?

88 DIFFICULTY ✪✪✪✪✪✪✪✪✪✪
Target time: 7 minutes

It's impossible to color in this shape so that no two colors touch without using four different colors. What is the LEAST number of times in which you have to resort to using the fourth color (i.e., on how many areas)?

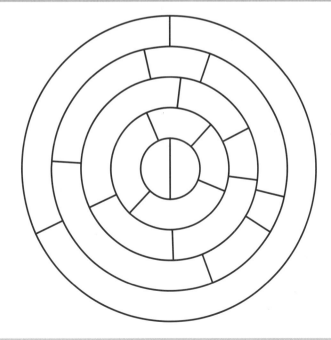

89 DIFFICULTY ✪✪✪✪✪☆☆☆☆☆
Target time: 4 minutes

In the puzzle below, which of the lettered squares (a, b, c, or d) fits into the empty space?

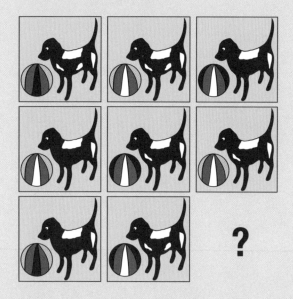

?

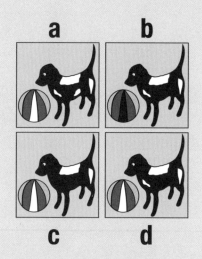

a   b

c   d

90 DIFFICULTY ✪✪✪☆☆☆☆☆☆☆
Target time: 4 minutes

Move one coin to make two rows of four in any direction.

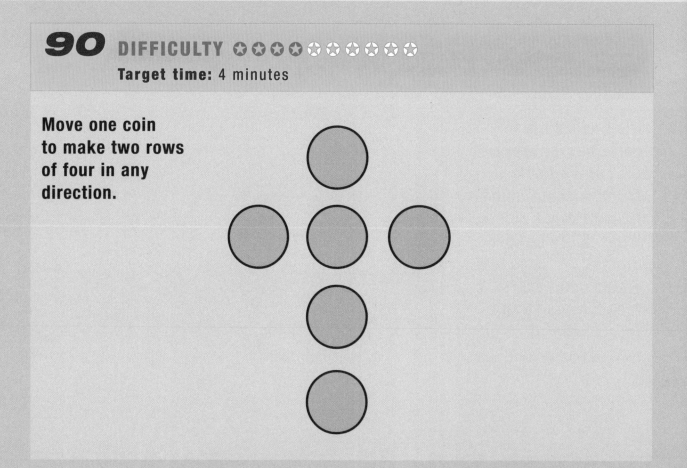

91

DIFFICULTY ✪✪✪✪✪✪✪✪✪✪

Target time: 10 minutes

Only two of these brick walls are identical. Can you determine which?

a

b

c

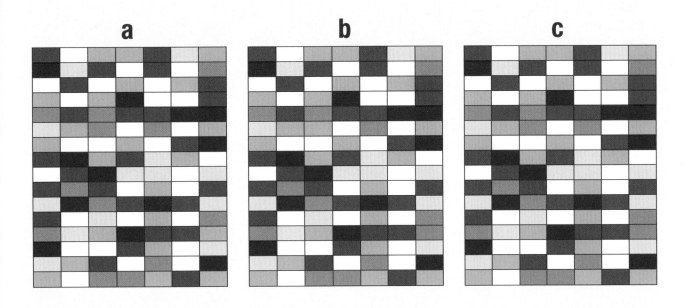

d

e

f

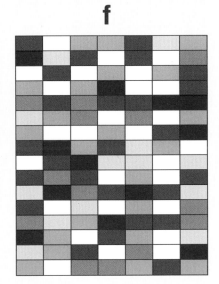

92 DIFFICULTY ★★★★★☆☆☆☆

Target time: 6 minutes

Can you spot the eight differences between these two pictures?
Circle them in the drawing on the right.

93 DIFFICULTY ★☆☆☆☆☆☆★★☆

Target time: 7 minutes

Which three pieces of cut flower will fit together
perfectly to form the flower seen on the right?

a

b

c

d

e

f

g

h

94 DIFFICULTY ✪✪✪✪☆☆☆☆☆☆
Target time: 5 minutes

Can you divide the clover leaf on the right by drawing two straight lines to produce four sections, each containing six different colors of flowers?

95 DIFFICULTY ✪✪✪✪✪☆☆☆☆☆
Target time: 3 minutes

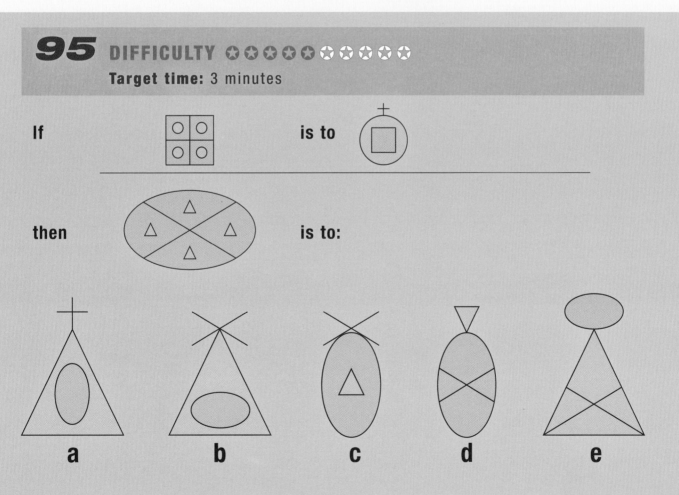

If _____ is to _____

then _____ is to:

a   b   c   d   e

96 DIFFICULTY ✪✪✪✪✪✪✪✪✪✪

Target time: 7 minutes

Bob the Baker was asked to make six identical cakes, but one didn't turn out quite as planned—which is different from the others?

a

b

c

d

e

f

97 DIFFICULTY ✪✪✪✪✪✪✪✪✪✪

Target time: 6 minutes

Which of the four boxed figures (a, b, c, or d) completes the set?

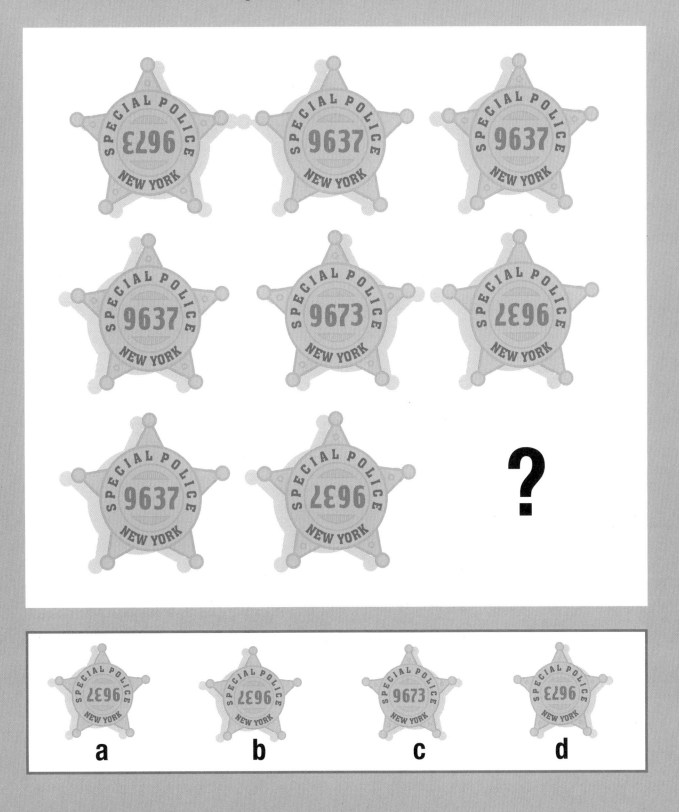

a   b   c   d

98 DIFFICULTY ✪✪✪✪✪✪✩✩✩✩

Target time: 5 minutes

Put three coins together so that they touch each other. Easy.

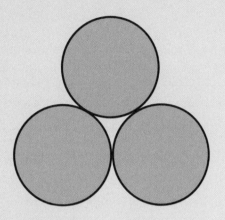

Now arrange four coins so they all touch. Not so difficult.

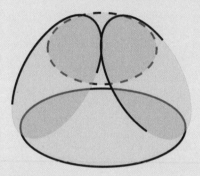

But can you arrange five so that they all touch?

99 DIFFICULTY ✪✪✪✪✪✪✪✩✩✩

Target time: 6 minutes

What is the value of the missing domino?

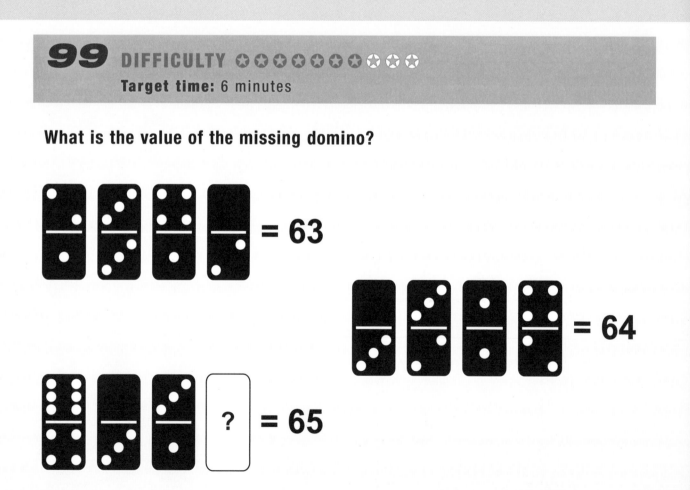

100 DIFFICULTY ✪✪✪✪✪✪✪✪✪✪

Target time: 7 minutes

Which four pieces of apple will fit together to form the apple below? Pieces may be rotated, but not flipped over.

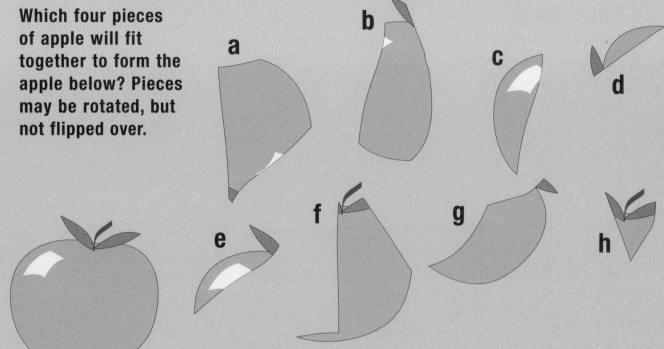

101 DIFFICULTY ✪✪✪✪✪✪✪✪✪✪

Target time: 4 minutes

In the sequence below, which of the lettered alternatives (a, b, c, or d) should replace the question mark?

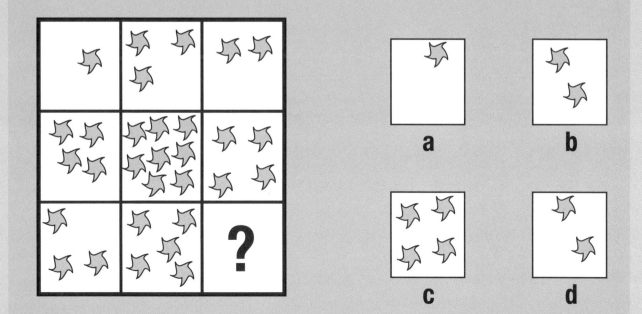

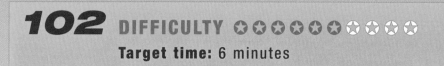

102 DIFFICULTY ✪✪✪✪✪✪☆☆☆☆

Target time: 6 minutes

Divide this sailing vessel by drawing three straight lines to produce four sections, each containing a ship's wheel, two anchors, and three ship's bells.

103 DIFFICULTY ✪✪✪✪✪✪✪✪☆☆

Target time: 5 minutes

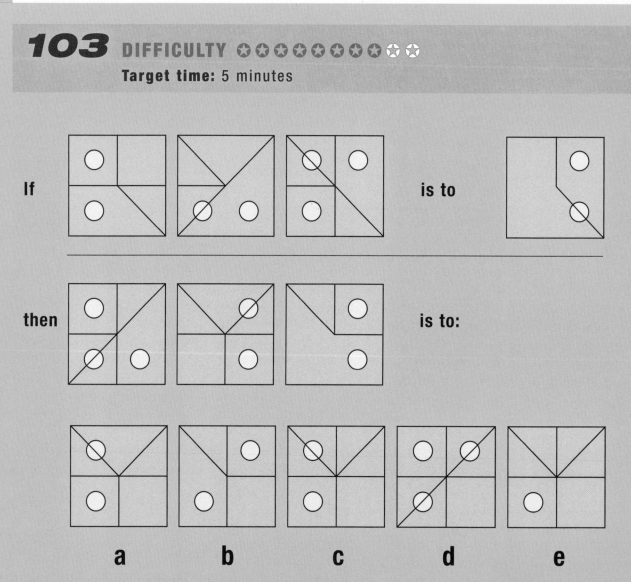

If ... is to ...

then ... is to:

a   b   c   d   e

104 DIFFICULTY ✪✪✪✪✪✪✪✪✪✪

Target time: 7 minutes

Florence played a game of Snakes and Ladders with her brother Tom. He threw the first 6, so started first, placing his playing piece on the 6. After that, every time it was Florence's turn, her die followed the sequence 6, 5, 4, 3, 2, 1, so her first move was to square 6, then square 11, etc. After his first turn when he threw the 6, Tom's die followed the sequence 1, 2, 3, 4, 5, 6 each time, so his second move was to square 7, his third was to 9, etc. The normal rules of the game were followed, so whenever someone lands on a square that has the foot of a ladder, the piece is moved to the top of the ladder. Whenever someone lands on a square that has the head of a snake, the piece is moved to the tail of the snake. The number thrown to end the game didn't necessarily matter, since the first person to move a piece completely off the board wins. Who won the game: Florence or Tom—or neither? If one or both children cannot win, can you see why?

FINISH

100	99	98	97	96	95	94	93	92	91
81	82	83	84	85	86	87	88	89	90
80	79	78	77	76	75	74	73	72	71
61	62	63	64	65	66	67	68	69	70
60	59	58	57	56	55	54	53	52	51
41	42	43	44	45	46	47	48	49	50
40	39	38	37	36	35	34	33	32	31
21	22	23	24	25	26	27	28	29	30
20	19	18	17	16	15	14	13	12	11
1	2	3	4	5	6	7	8	9	10

START

105 DIFFICULTY ✪✪✪✪✪✪☆☆☆

Target time: 7 minutes

Only two of these tea canisters are exactly identical.
Can you determine which two?

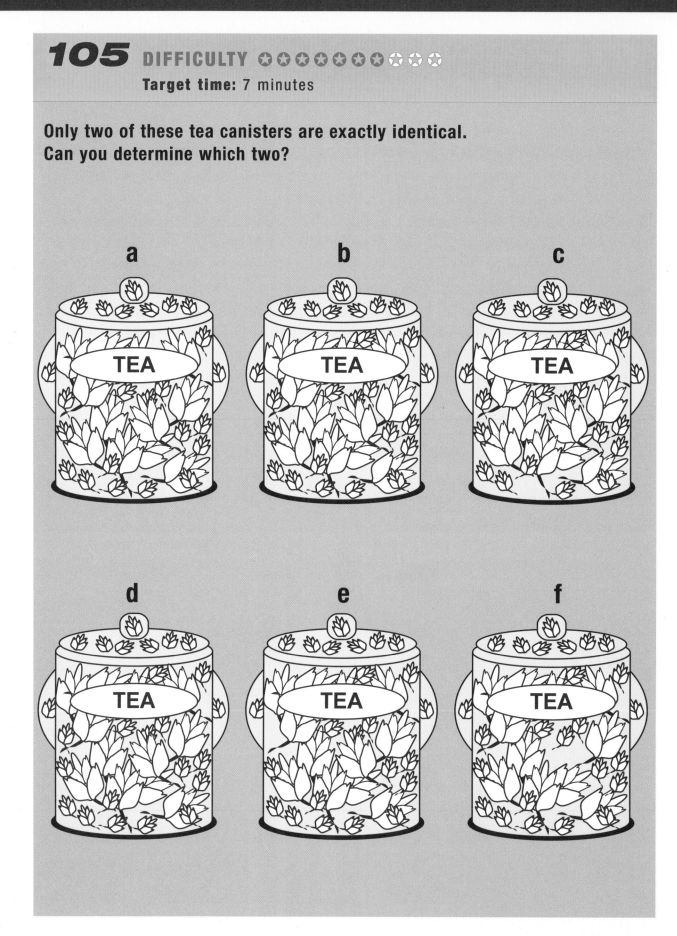

106 DIFFICULTY ✪✪✪✪✪✪✪✪✪✪
Target time: 5 minutes

In the sequence below, which of the lettered alternatives (a, b, c, or d) should replace the question mark?

```
L A D
P C F
Y K W
```

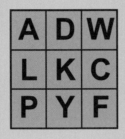
```
A D W
L K C
P Y F
```

```
D W F
A Y K
L P C
```

?

```
C F W
Y P D
K L A
```
a

```
Y F D
K C A
W P L
```
b

```
W F C
D Y P
A K L
```
c

```
W F C
D P Y
A L K
```
d

107 DIFFICULTY ✪✪✪✪✪✪✪✪✪✪
Target time: 10 minutes

Place the given dominoes into the spaces in the grid on the right in such a way that the number of dots in each of the four horizontal rows totals eighteen, and the number of dots in each of the six vertical columns totals twelve.

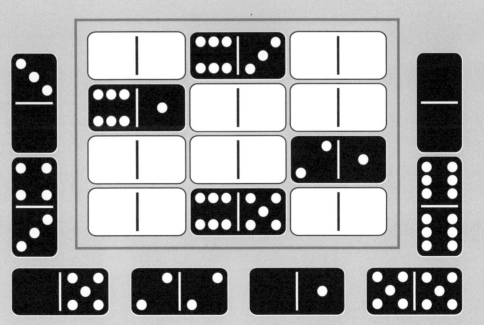

108 DIFFICULTY ✪✪✪✪✪✪✪✪✪✪

Target time: 8 minutes

Which shapes go in the highlighted rectangle to complete the hidden sequence?

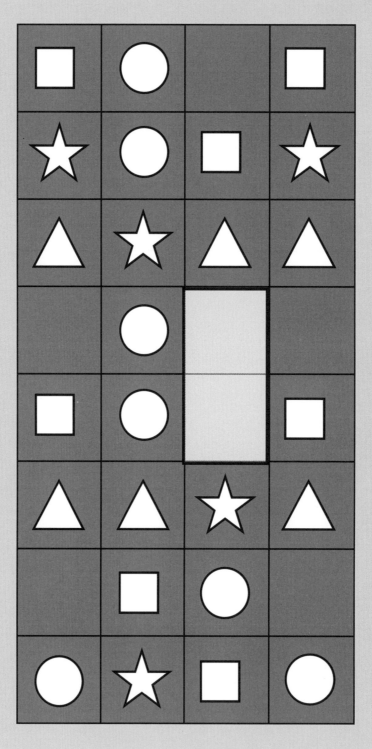

109 DIFFICULTY ✪✪✪✪✪✪✪✪✪

Target time: 10 minutes

Make your way from a to b through this honeycomb maze.

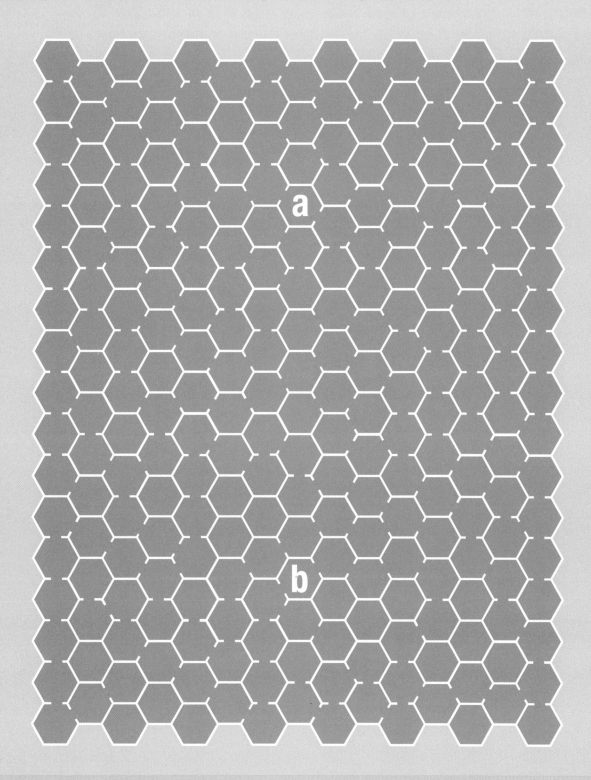

110 DIFFICULTY ✪✪✪✪✪✪✪✪✪

Target time: 10 minutes

Young Bill the builder has been busy. In each of the four buildings below, one brick is used more or less frequently than it is in the other three buildings. Can you determine the different brick in each construction? The ten brick types are as follows:

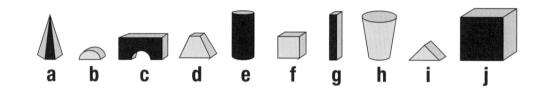

a   b   c   d   e   f   g   h   i   j

Building 1

Building 2

Building 3

Building 4

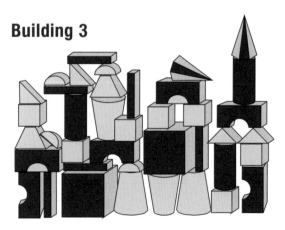

111 DIFFICULTY ✪✪✪✪✪✪✪☆☆☆

Target time: 20 minutes

Wait till you "sea" how this nonogram turns out! (See page 11 for advice on how to complete a nonogram.)

112 DIFFICULTY ✪✪✪✪✪✪✪✪✪✪

Target time: 5 minutes

When the shape below is folded to form a cube, which one of the following (a, b, c, d, or e) is produced?

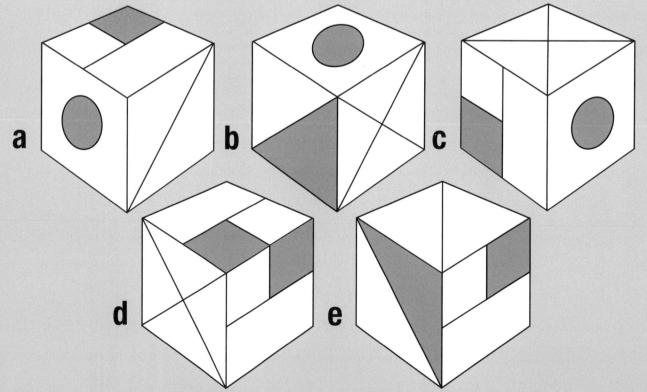

113 DIFFICULTY ✪✪✪✪✪☆☆☆☆☆
Target time: 5 minutes

Can you spot the ten differences between these two pictures? Circle them in the drawing on the right.

114 DIFFICULTY ✪✪✪✪✪✪✪☆☆☆
Target time: 7 minutes

Connect all five pairs of like dots with continuous unbroken lines. All the lines run up, down, left, or right along the grid lines— none is a diagonal. No two lines should cross or touch, even at corners.

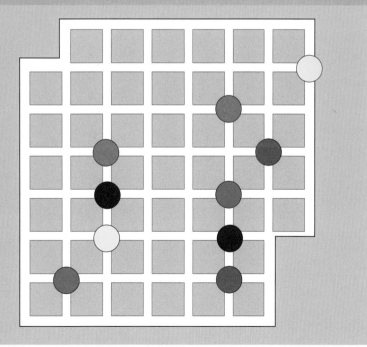

115 DIFFICULTY ✪✪✪✪✪✪✪☆☆

Target time: 7 minutes

Divide this picture by
drawing four straight lines
to produce five sections,
each containing five different
household items from a
possible choice of seven.

116 DIFFICULTY ✪✪✪☆☆☆☆☆☆☆

Target time: 3 minutes

In the octagonal
sequence shown on
the right, which of
the alternatives
(a, b, c, d, or e)
should replace
the missing piece
from this curious-
looking pie?

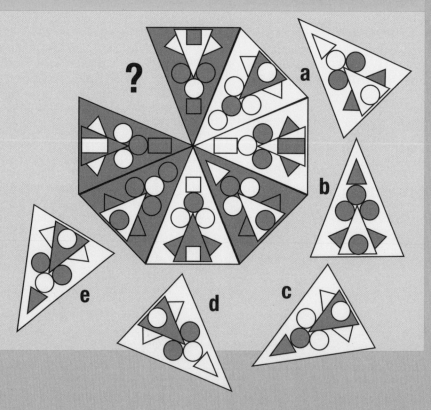

117 DIFFICULTY ✪✪✪✪✪✪✩✩✩

Target time: 7 minutes

Below are six identical jigsaw puzzles, each with a piece missing.
Can you determine which of the numbered pieces is needed to
complete each puzzle?

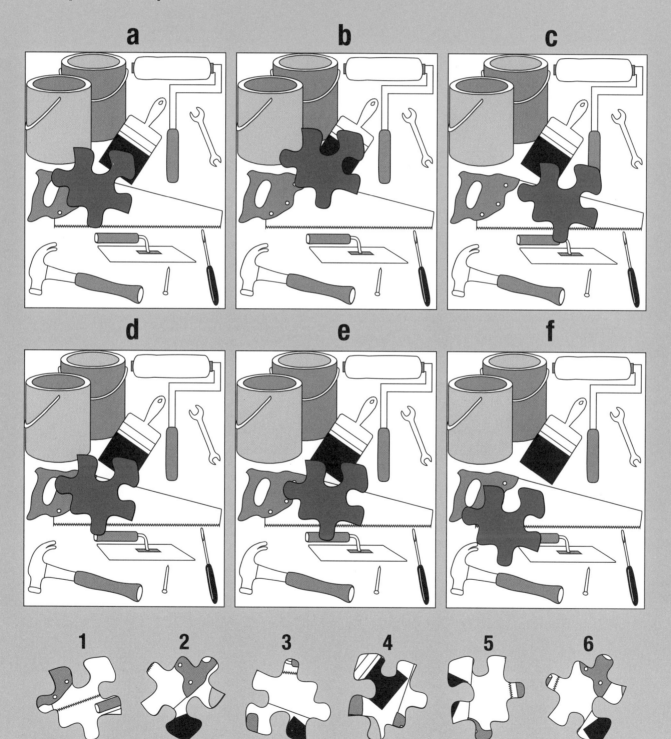

118 DIFFICULTY ✪✪✪✪✪✪✪✩✩✩
Target time: 5 minutes

Match the eight arrow flights with the correct arrowheads. If you pick the correct ones, an appropriate word will be spelled out.

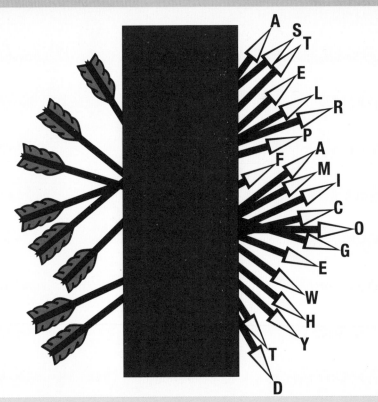

119 DIFFICULTY ✪✪✪✪✪✪✪✩✩✩
Target time: 7 minutes

Can you spot the ten differences between these two pictures? Circle them in the drawing on the right.

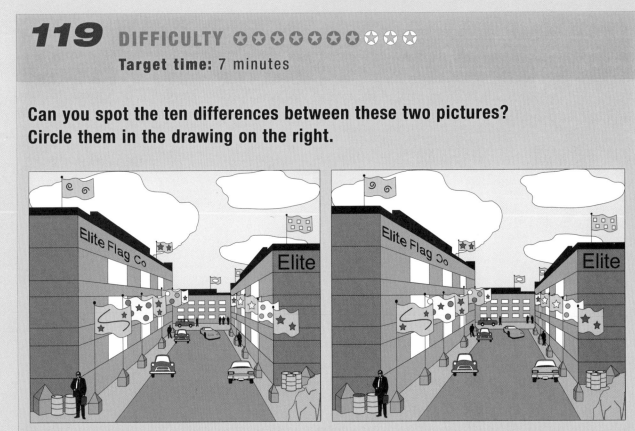

120

DIFFICULTY ✪✪✪✪✪✩✩✩✩✩

Target time: 3 minutes

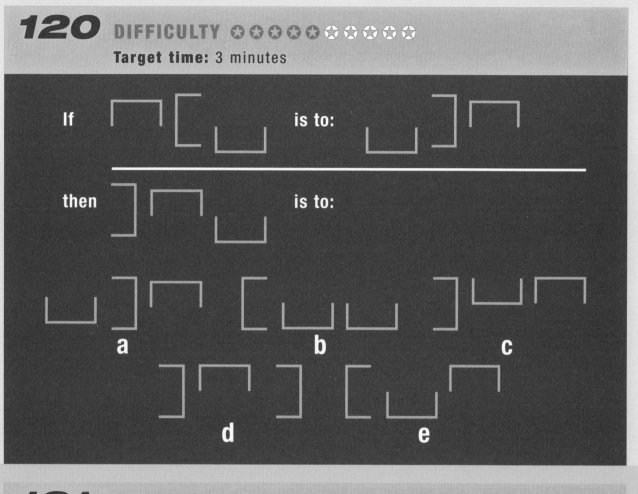

If [shape] is to:

then [shape] is to:

a   b   c

d   e

121

DIFFICULTY ✪✪✪✪✪✪✪✩✩

Target time: 5 minutes

In the puzzle below, which of the lettered squares (a, b, c, or d) fits into the empty space?

?

a   b

c   d

122 DIFFICULTY ✪✪✪✪✪✪✪✪✪✪

Target time: 6 minutes

You can't tell which way up these coins are just by touch, but you do know that half are heads and half are tails-side up. Can you, while blindfolded, divide them into two piles so that each pile has the same number of coins heads-side up?

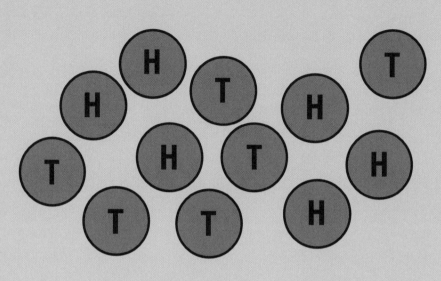

123 DIFFICULTY ✪✪✪✪✪✪✪✪✪✪

Target time: 10 minutes

The archaeologists at the museum of antiquities are having a hard time piecing together six pots they discovered at a recent dig. Can you match the correct missing piece with each vase to finish the task?

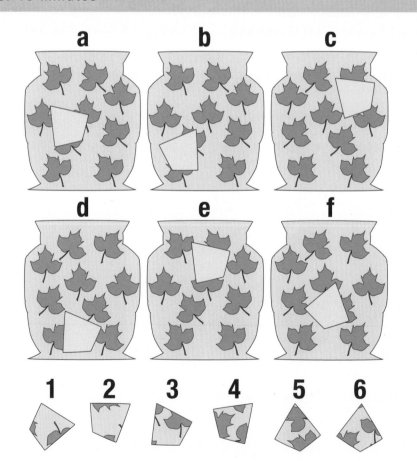

124 DIFFICULTY ✪✪✪✪✪✪✪☆☆☆
Target time: 7 minutes

Can you divide the picture on the right by drawing three straight lines to produce four sections, each containing different quantities (six, seven, eight, and ten) of assorted shapes? No section contains more than one of each shape.

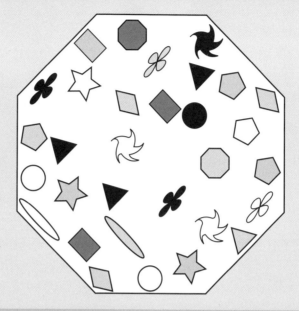

125 DIFFICULTY ✪✪✪✪✪✪✪✪☆☆
Target time: 6 minutes

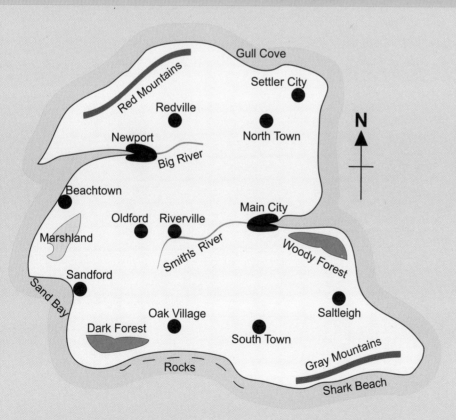

Study this map of an island for one minute, then see if you can answer the questions on page 100 without checking back.

[125] DIFFICULTY ✪✪✪✪✪✪✪✪✪✪

Target time: 6 minutes

Can you answer these questions about the puzzle on page 99 without checking back?

1. Which town lies directly west of North Town?

2. Which mountain range is furthest south?

3. On which river does Riverville stand?

4. What geographical feature is directly west of Oldford?

5. Which town or city is furthest north?

6. Which town or city is furthest east?

7. Which river runs through Newport?

8. Which is the nearest forest to Sand Bay?

126 DIFFICULTY ✪✪✪✪✪✪✪✪✪✪

Target time: 2 minutes

Which number should replace the question mark?

 = 11

= 50

 = 24

= ?

127 DIFFICULTY ✪✪✪✪✪✪✪✪✪✪

Target time: 10 minutes

Can you pair each of the stamps with its correct print?

128 DIFFICULTY ✪✪✪✪✪✪✩✩✩✩

Target time: 6 minutes

Divide this picture by drawing four straight lines to produce six sections, each containing six different shapes in six different colors.

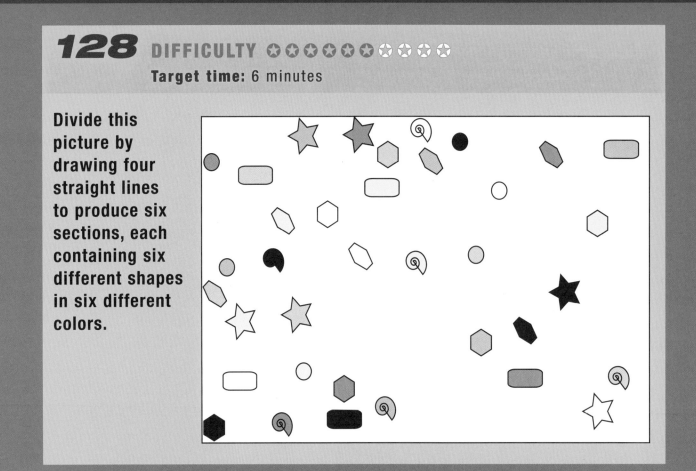

129 DIFFICULTY ✪✪✪✪✪✪✪✩✩✩

Target time: 7 minutes

Can you pair these door keys with the impressions of their ends? Take care though—first impressions may not be what they seem—some could be mirror images!

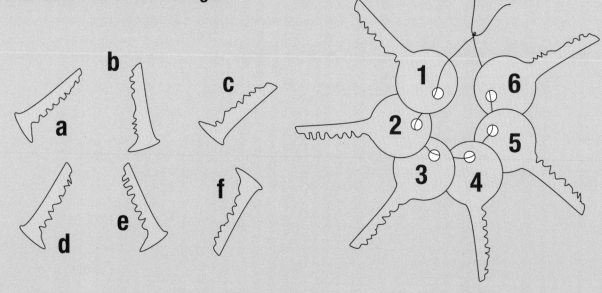

130 DIFFICULTY ✪✪✪✪✪✪✪✪✪✪

Target time: 7 minutes

This shape can be folded up to make a cube with a single continuous line around it. But there's been a mistake. Which face is wrong? Can you tell without making the cube? Can you also tell what should be on that face to make the line continuous?

131 DIFFICULTY ✪✪✪✪✪✪✪✪✪

Target time: 7 minutes

In the sequence below, which of the lettered alternatives (a, b, c, or d) should replace the question mark?

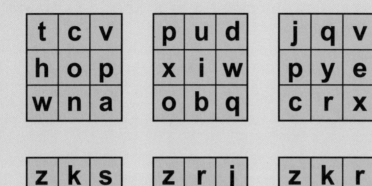

t	c	v
h	o	p
w	n	a

p	u	d
x	i	w
o	b	q

j	q	v
p	y	e
c	r	x

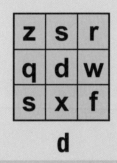

?

z	k	s
r	w	t
j	p	d

a

z	r	j
d	q	v
s	y	f

b

z	k	r
d	q	w
s	y	f

c

z	s	r
q	d	w
s	x	f

d

132 DIFFICULTY ✪✪✪✪✪✪✪✪✪

Target time: 4 minutes

In the sequence below, which of the lettered alternatives (a, b, c, or d) should replace the question mark?

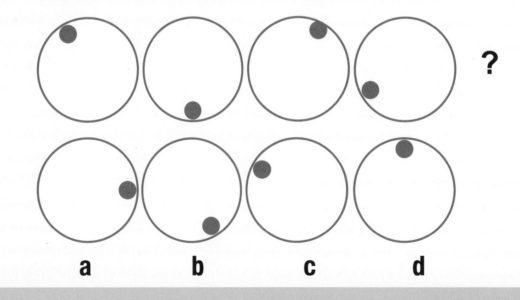

?

a   **b**   **c**   **d**

133 DIFFICULTY ✪✪✪✪✪✪✪✪✪✪
Target time: 10 minutes

Tom and Jim have been busy building walls. In each of the four walls below, one brick is used more or less frequently than it is in the other three walls. Can you determine the different brick in each construction? The ten brick types are as follows:

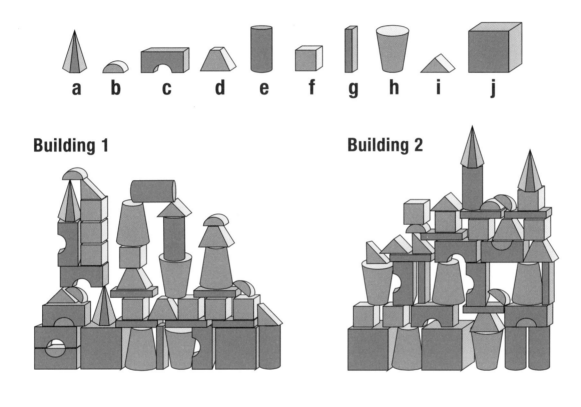

a   b   c   d   e   f   g   h   i   j

Building 1

Building 2

Building 3

Building 4

1

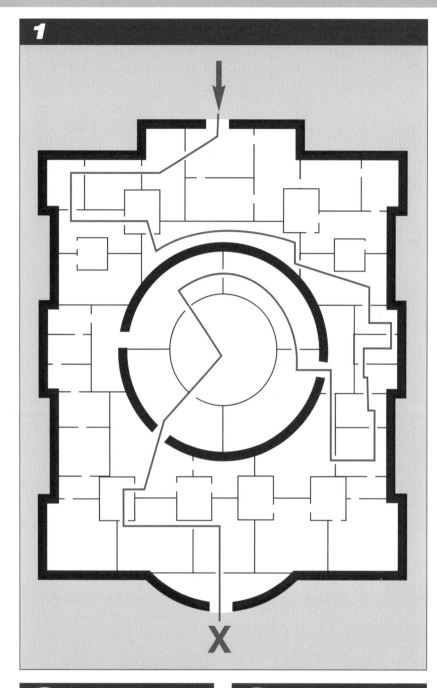

4

5

Twelve; the opposite sides of a die add up to seven, so the bottom three faces are (from left to right) two spots, four spots, and six spots, thus a total of twelve.

6

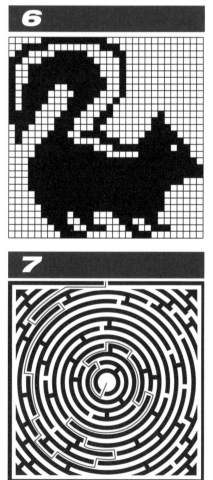

2

Whatever move your opponent performs, make the diametrically opposite move on your next turn. For example, if your opponent takes the coin in the top left corner, you take the coin in the bottom right corner.

3

1. 2
2. 1
3. 0
4. 0
5. 3
6. 2 + 1 = 3
7. 1 + 1 = 2
8. 12

7

8

d; each line contains two white stars and a yellow star, and each line also has a circled star. Each line contains a red and blue halved circle that has been turned through 0 degrees, 90 degrees, and 180 degrees (resulting in two lines running from top to bottom and one line from side to side). The missing image should contain a white star and a circle that has been turned through 90 degrees (i.e., runs from side to side).

9

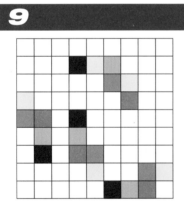

10

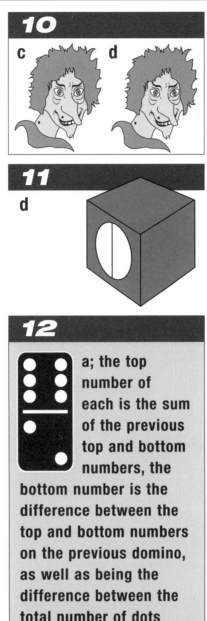

c   d

11

d

12

a; the top number of each is the sum of the previous top and bottom numbers, the bottom number is the difference between the top and bottom numbers on the previous domino, as well as being the difference between the total number of dots on both dominoes.

13

Twenty-three; Angelica can see the top faces of all three dice, thus a total of twelve spots. The opposite sides of a die add up to seven. On the furthest left die, the side face Angelica can see has two spots. On the central die, the side face Angelica can see has three spots. On the furthest right die, the side face Angelica can see has five spots. On the bottom face of the furthest right die, there are four spots, and the end face of this die (invisible to you) doesn't have six spots (intro), so must have one. Thus Angelica can see a total of twelve spots on the top faces, ten spots on the side faces and one on the end face, so a combined total of twenty-three spots.

14

One spot. ⊙
To determine why, look at each row, either going from side to side or on a diagonal from right to left or left to right. In each of these three possible directions, the row must contain all odd-numbered circles or all even-numbered circles. Going from right to left (or vice versa) the row in which the middle circle appears contains a five spot and a one spot, so it follows that the middle circle must contain another odd spot (in this case a one). Similarly, from bottom right to top left, the row contains a one, another odd number.

15

e; (it has more diamonds toward the nib of the pen).

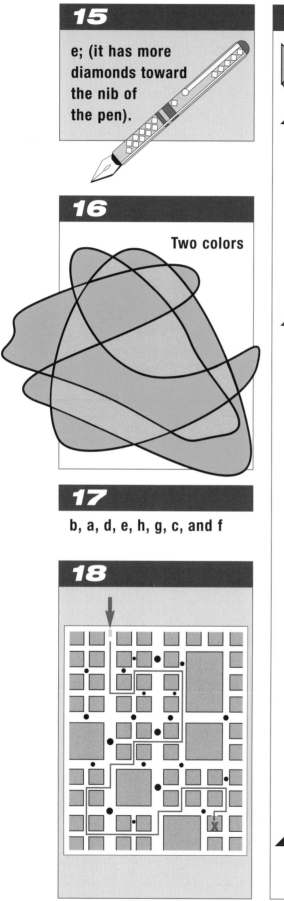

16

Two colors

17

b, a, d, e, h, g, c, and f

18

19

a

b

c

d

e

f

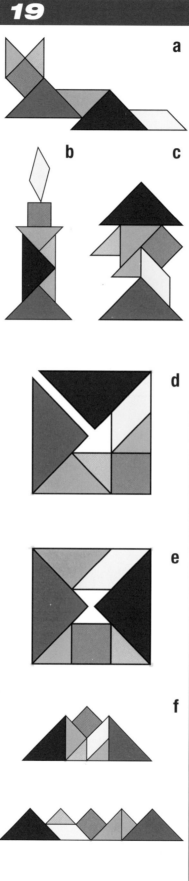

20

b

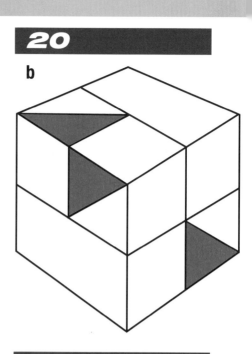

21

b; each line contains one dog with a white ear, two dogs with a patched eye, and two dogs with their tongues out. The missing image must have a white patched eye, no white ear, and its tongue hanging out.

22

a and c

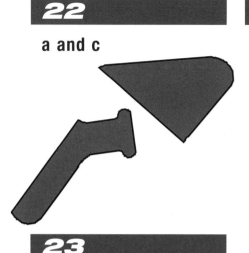

23

b; the total number of dots increases in number first by one, then by two, then by three, and finally by four, so the final number of dots must equal twelve.

24

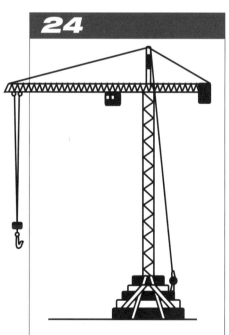

a; the struts at the base are closer together and do not extend to the outside edge of the base.

25

Each square contains a symbol with one side more or one side less than its immediate neighbor (above, below, left, right). Each symbol is also a color with one letter in its name more or one letter less than its immediate neighbor, e.g., red, blue, green, yellow, apricot.

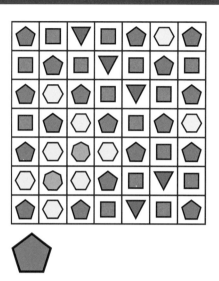

26

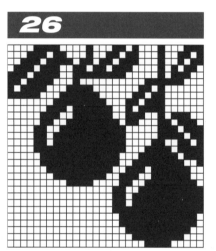

27

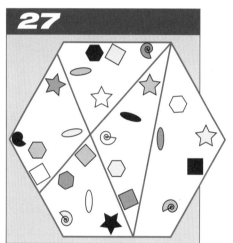

28

Four colors are needed.

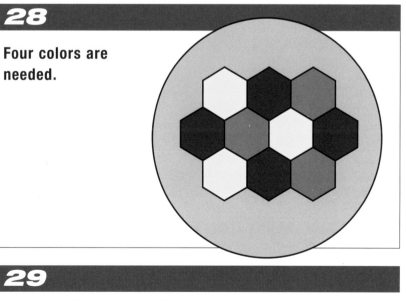

29

a = 4, b = 6, c = 3, d = 7, e = 2, f = 1, and g = 5

30

Domino 3/3 must be used with a 3 at the other corner and since there is only one other 3 (attached to a 1, totaling 4), the next corner is a 5. There is only one 5 (attached to a 2), so the corner is 2. Since the remaining corner of this side is a 3, this must be domino 2/4. Thus (similarly any rotation or reflection):

Domino 1/2 must be used with a 6 at the corner. This is attached to the 2, which requires a corner domino of 1, so 1/4. The corner of this side must be 4, part of domino 4/4, so this is next to corner 1, part of domino 1/2. Thus (similarly any rotation or reflection):

31

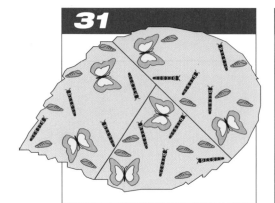

32

1. Pink
2. Red
3. 3
4. 3
5. 1
6. 2
7. 3
8. 4

34

c; each line contains two tic-tac-toe games where Xs win and one where Os win.
Each line contains a pink, an orange, and a blue square.
Each line contains two white games and a yellow game.
The winning game must therefore have an X win, a pink square, and a yellow game.

33

35

a

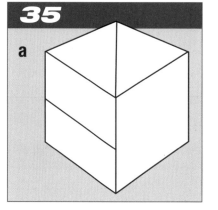

36

a and d

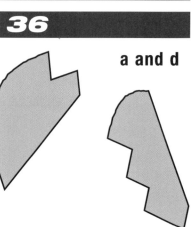

37

Start:

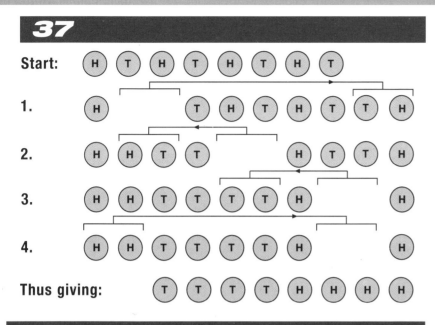

Thus giving:

38

The number in square 31 isn't 6 (clue 2), so in diagonal 6–31, square 21 = 6. Square 36 isn't 3 (clue 3), so in diagonal 1–36, square 15 = 3; and in 6–36, 24 = 3. Square 31 is 5 or 2 (2) as is 32 (1), so 36 is neither, thus 36 = 6 and 25 = 6 (3). Square 8 isn't 6 (diagonal), so in 2–32, square 2 = 6; thus 10 = 6. In 13–18, the 1 isn't in 14 (2), so must be in 13. Since there's a 5 in 22, there isn't a 5 in 1 or 19, so in 1–31, 31 = 5; so 14 = 5 (2), 32 = 2, and 3 = 2 (1). By elimination, 1 = 4, 8 = 1, 19 = 2, 20 = 4, 9 = 5, 27 = 1, 29 = 2 (diagonal), 11 = 4 (diagonal), 16 = 2, 28 = 4, 30 = 5, 4 = 3, 5 = 5, 12 = 2, 18 = 4, 23 = 1, 35 = 3, and 34 = 1.

4	6	2	3	5	1
3	1	5	6	4	2
1	5	3	2	6	4
2	4	6	5	1	3
6	3	1	4	2	5
5	2	4	1	3	6

39

11:35; the hour hand moves back by four hours (or forward by eight hours) and the minute hand moves forward by seven minutes each time.

40

b

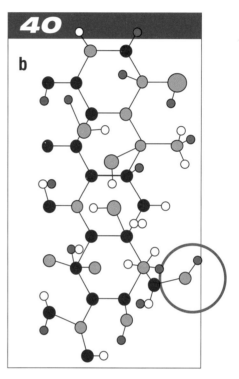

41

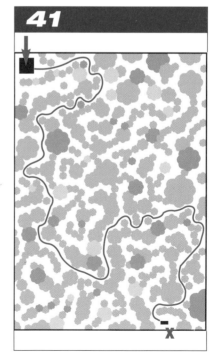

42

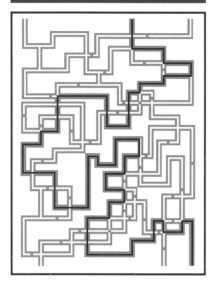

43

It is possible to do with three colors.

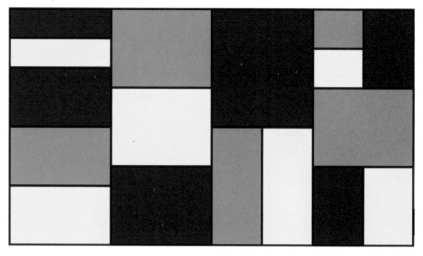

44

1	5	4	6	3	2
2	3	6	5	1	4
6	1	2	3	4	5
3	2	5	4	6	1
4	6	1	2	5	3
5	4	3	1	2	6

The number in row four, column four cannot be 1 or 2 (horizontal) or 3 or 5 (diagonal) or 6 (vertical), so it must be 4. Similarly, row six, column six cannot be 1, 2, 3, 4, or 5, so it must be 6. To complete the diagonal column one, row one must be 1. In row four, the 5 cannot be in column one or five, so it must be column three. The total of the four corner spots is 14 (intro) so row one, column six is 2. The top right to bottom left

diagonal contains five different numbers and no 4, so row three, column four is not 2, 4, 5, or 6 so it must be 1 or 3. As neither row five, column two nor row two, column five can be a 3, row three, column four must be 3. Column six, row three must be 5, and row five 3. In row one, the 5 cannot be in column three or five, so it must be in column two. In column five, the 2 cannot be in rows one, three, or four so it must be in row six. In row six, the 3 cannot be in columns two or four so must be in column three, the 4 cannot be in column four so must be in column two, which leaves 1 in column four. The 5 in column four cannot be in row five, so it must be in row two, and

the 2 in row five. In row two, the 2 cannot be in column three or five so it must be in column one. In column one, the 3 cannot be in rows three or five, so it must be in row four. Thus row four, column five is 6. In row one, the 3 is not in column three, so it must be in column five, and the 4 in column three. In row two the 6 is not in column five so it must be in column three, and the 1 in column five. Column five is thus completed by a 4 in row three. In row three, the 1 is not in column one, so it must be in column two, and the 6 in column one. Thus column one is completed by a 4, column two by a 6, and column three by a 1.

45

1

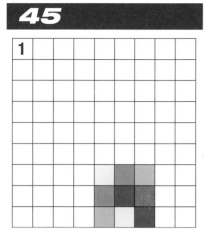

2

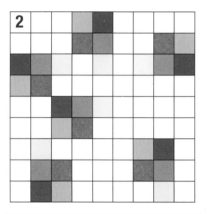

46

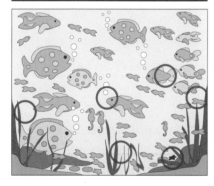

47

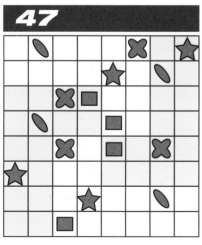

48

b and e

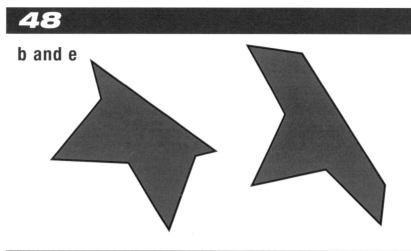

49

Two dominoes each total 9 (5/4 and 6/3). For these sides to total 10, both 1s must be corner numbers. Two dominoes each total 7 (5/2 and 4/3). They must each have 3 as a corner number, thus 3/4 and 3/6 (as 3/1 has a corner of 1, as described above). So one square has domino 3/4 with the 3 as a corner and the 3 of 3/6 as its other corner to total 10. Domino 3/6 must have 1 at its corner. If the 1 domino is 1/3, the corner is 6, thus 6/2 (6/3 has been used) but the final side would then total 11, which is incorrect. So the domino is 1/4, with 5 at the corner, hence 5/2 to make the correct total (see image below left).

The remaining dominoes form a square with domino 5/4 and a corner of 1, part of domino 1/3. To total 10, 1/3 has a corner of 6 from domino 6/2. which in turn has a corner of 2 from domino 2/4 (see image above right).

50

The bottom one. This results in the domino squares alternating between odd and even in rows and columns (except the fifth row, which is now incomplete).

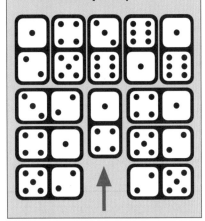

51

a and c

52

The shortest route is thirty moves, as follows: 2 to x, 6 to 2, 5 to a, x to 5, a to 6, 2 to c, 1 to x, c to 1, 6 to 2, 7 to a, 8 to b, 5 to 8, b to 5, x to 7, a to 6, 2 to c, 3 to x, 4 to b, 1 to 4, b to 1, c to 3, 6 to 2, 5 to a, x to 5, a to 6, 2 to c, 1 to x, c to 1, 6 to 2, x to 6.

53

54

a; the large star rotates by a quarter turn counterclockwise, and the smaller shapes within it by a quarter turn clockwise every time.

55

56

c; the total number of dots increases in number by two every time.

57

c and d

58

a and g are the same.

59

1d; each line contains two airships with red fins and one with blue fins. Each line contains two airships with red gondolas underneath and one with a blue gondola. Each line contains two airships facing left and one facing right. Each line contains two airships with four lights on the balloon and one with three lights. The missing image therefore has blue fins, a red gondola, faces left, and has four lights on the balloon, so it must be d.

60

Push the middle row up by moving the top coin to the bottom and using it to push up the whole column.

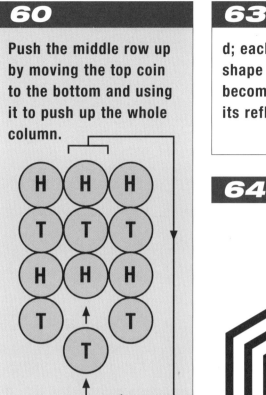

61

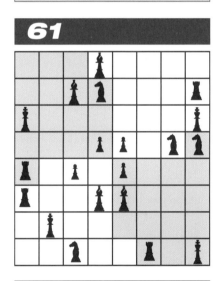

62

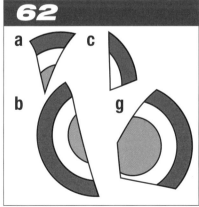

63

d; each shape becomes its reflection.

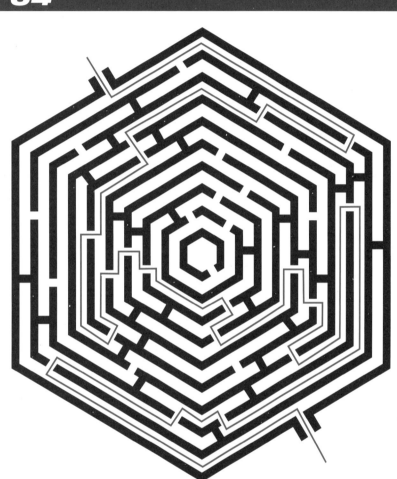

64

65

1. Orange
2. Orange
3. 2
4. 3
5. 3
6. 2
7. 3
8. Orange

66

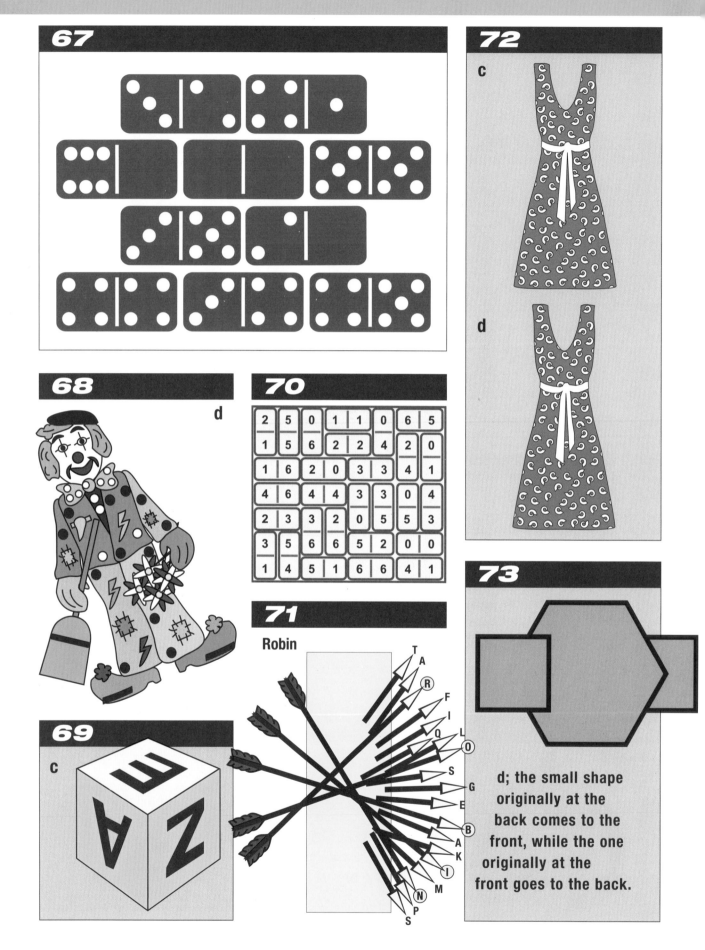

67

68

d

69

c

70

2	5	0	1	1	0	6	5
1	5	6	2	2	4	2	0
1	6	2	0	3	3	4	1
4	6	4	4	3	3	0	4
2	3	3	2	0	5	5	3
3	5	6	6	5	2	0	0
1	4	5	1	6	6	4	1

71

Robin

72

c

d

73

d; the small shape originally at the back comes to the front, while the one originally at the front goes to the back.

74

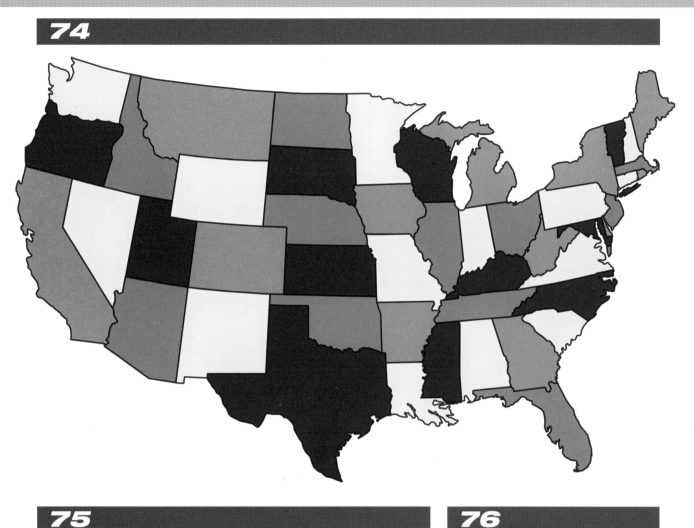

75

a; each line contains two signs that are right-side up, and one that is upside-down. Each line contains two "STOP"s with an exclamation point and one without. Each line contains one red "FILTERED" and two black. On each line the steam is colored white twice and yellow once. The missing image should be right-side up. "STOP" should have an exclamation point. "FILTERED" should be in black. The steam on the cup should be yellow, so it must be a.

76

77

Since the opposite two sides of a die have spots totaling seven, Peter gave double the quantity of the number of spots that appear on the opposite side of the die. The yellow die relates to the quantity of loaves, and the blue to the quantity of fish. Thus Mary was awarded four loaves and ten fish.

78

82

Pattern a can be found six times.

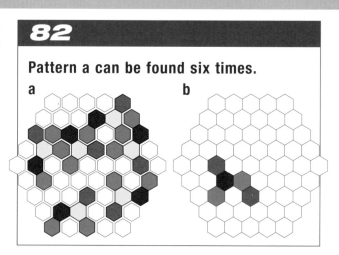

79

1. Barry
2. Roger
3. Tom
4. White
5. 5
6. 4

7. 3
   (Katie, Jane,
   and Anna)
8. 3
   (Will, Mary,
   and Jane)

80

1. e
and f
2. g
3. 3
4. 1
5. 1

6. 8
7. 1
8. 30

83

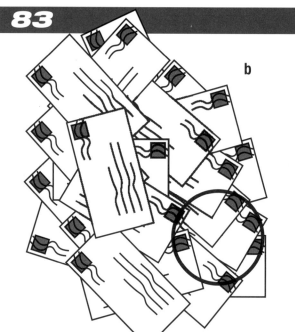

b

81

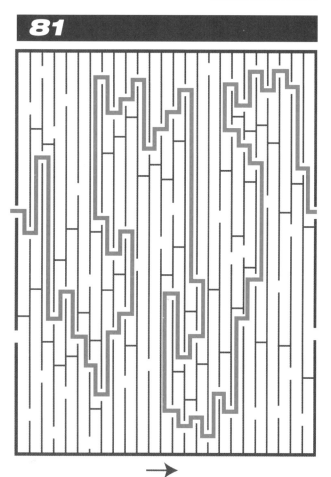

→

84

85

d

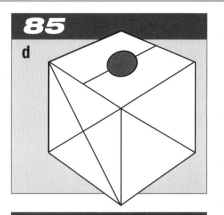

86

Tom

87

Green. Each set of four triangles has 3 colors.

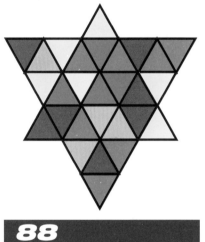

88

You need to resort to using it only once.

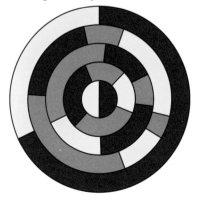

89

b; each different dog and each different ball appears three times. Thus the missing dog has three white spots and a ball with two green stripes, two red stripes, and one black stripe.

90

One answer is to place the topmost coin on top of the one at the center of the cross.

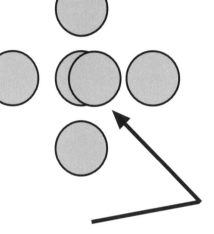

91

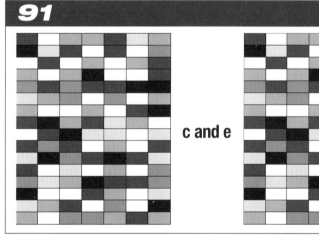

c and e

92

93

b

g

c

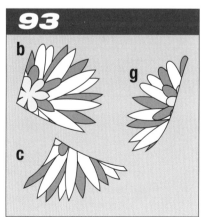

94

95

b; the four small triangles merge into one triangle that increases in size. The cross originally in the ellipse goes on top of the triangle. The ellipse reduces in size and goes inside the triangle.

96

f

97

c; each line contains two badges with the number 9637 and one with the number 9673.

Each line contains two badges with the number right-side up and one with it upside-down.
Each line contains one badge with the circles on the points of the star removed. Each line contains two badges where the shadow falls to the left and one where it falls to the right.

The missing image should have the number 9673 and be right-side up. The circles on the points of the star should be intact and the shadow should fall to the right, so it must be c.

98

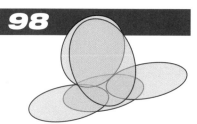

Place two coins on top of one coin, then balance another two coins so that they support each other and touch the three coins lying flat.

99

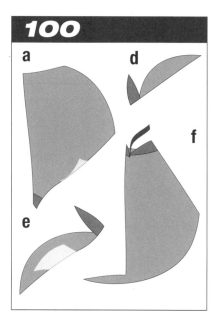

The missing domino is 0/1; the figure is derived by adding the total dots on the first two dominoes and multiplying the answer by the total dots on the second two dominoes.

100

101

b; reading across any row or down any column, the sum of the outer two squares is equal to that of the inner square, so the missing square must have two shapes.

102

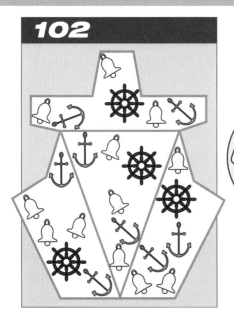

103

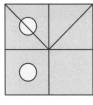

c; only lines that appear in the same position just twice in the first three squares are carried forward to the final square. Only circles that appear just once are carried forward.

104

Tom can win, but Florence can't. Eventually, Florence reaches a point where she throws a 5 and lands on square 64. From there, her moves are: 68–87, 90, 92–72, 73, 79, 84–64, 68–87, 90, 92–72, 73, 79, 84–64, 68–87, 90, 92–72, etc.; thus her moves never get beyond square 92.

105

b and d

106

d; each letter moves one place along in the direction of the arrow, as shown.

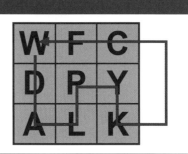

107

In the middle column of complete dominoes, the left-hand side of the missing dominoes must both be 0, and the right-hand sides are 1 + 3. In the third

horizontal row from the top, the central right-hand side of the middle domino can't be 1, so this domino is 0/3, thus 0/1 is the middle domino in the second row. The domino furthest right in the second horizontal row from the top is 5/5, thus the domino furthest left in the third row from the top is 6/6. The left-hand vertical column of complete dominoes has 0/0 and 0/5, so 0/0 is in the bottom row, and 0/5 in the top row. Domino 2/2 is in the top row, and the domino in the bottom row furthest right position is 3/4.

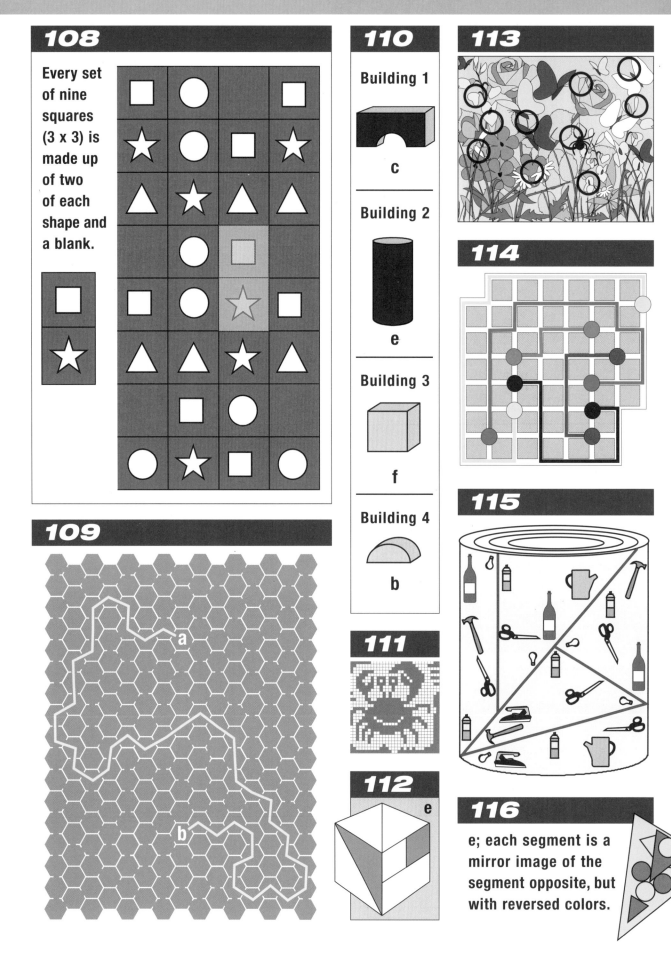

108

Every set of nine squares (3 x 3) is made up of two of each shape and a blank.

109

110

Building 1

c

Building 2

e

Building 3

f

Building 4

b

111

112

e

113

114

115

116

e; each segment is a mirror image of the segment opposite, but with reversed colors.

117

a = 2, b = 4, c = 3,
d = 6, e = 5, f = 1

118

Straight

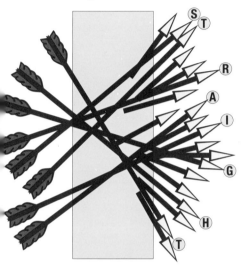

119

120

 e; in each case the shape becomes a reflection of itself.

121

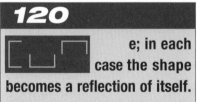 d; from left to right in each horizontal row, the lowest book moves to the top of the pile; and from top to bottom, in each vertical column, the two lowest books move to the top of the pile.

122

Divide the coins into two piles without turning any over. Then turn over every coin in one of the piles. Try it and see!

123

a = 4, b = 5, c = 1, d = 2, e = 6, f = 3

124

125

1. Redville
2. Gray Mountains
3. Smith's River
4. Marshland
5. Settler City
6. Saltleigh
7. Big River
8. Dark Forest

126

63; multiply the total number of dots on the first domino by the total number of dots on the second.

127

1 = d, 2 = a, 3 = e, 4 = b, 5 = c, 6 = f

128

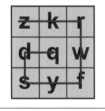

129

1 = c, 2 = e, 3 = f, 4 = a, 5 = d, 6 = b

130

When the original cutout shape is made into a cube there are two continuous lines. To have only one, there should be two horizontal lines on the face on the bottom of the diagram instead of two semicircles.

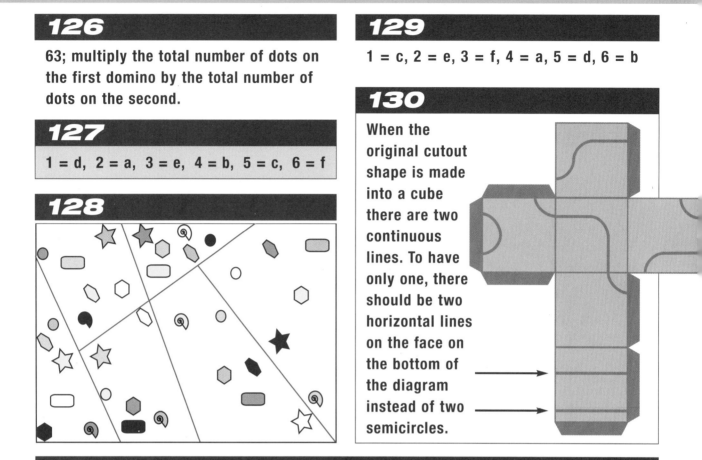

131

c; each letter moves one place on in the alphabet, then the central letter moves to the top left-hand corner, while the others move one place forward in the direction of the arrow, as shown.

132

a; think of this as being like a clock where the circle represents an hour number on the face—the hour moves back five places every time, so ends up at "3 o'clock," which is a.

133

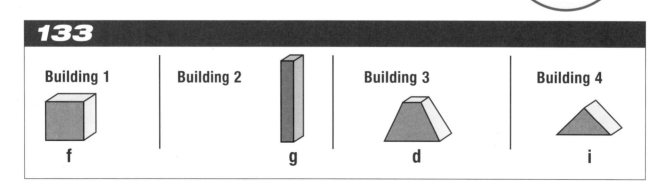

Building 1
f

Building 2
g

Building 3
d

Building 4
i

ACKNOWLEDGMENTS ✪ PERCEPTUAL PUZZLERS

✪ Puzzle contributors

Contributors are listed next to the numbers of the puzzles they created.

✪ Brainwarp

Puzzles 14, 25, 37, 50, 60, 87, 90, 98, 108, 122, 130

✪ David Bodycombe

Puzzles 2, 9, 16, 19, 28, 43, 45, 52, 71, 74, 82, 88, 114, 118

✪ Guy Campbell

Puzzles 1, 7, 8, 18, 21, 34, 41, 42, 59, 64, 75, 81, 97, 109

✪ Philip Carter & Ken Russell

Puzzles 11, 20, 35, 63, 69, 85, 95, 103, 112, 120

✪ Puzzlemakers

Puzzles 3, 4, 5, 6, 10, 12, 13, 15, 17, 22, 23, 24, 26, 27, 29, 30, 31, 32, 33, 36, 38, 39, 40, 44, 46, 47, 48, 49, 51, 53, 54, 55, 56, 57, 58, 61, 62, 65, 66, 67, 68, 70, 72, 73, 76, 77, 78, 79, 80, 83, 84, 86, 89, 91, 92, 93, 94, 96, 99, 100, 101, 102, 104, 105, 106, 107, 110, 111, 113, 115, 116, 117, 119, 121, 123, 124, 125, 126, 127, 128, 129, 131, 132, 133

Perceptual Puzzlers was commissioned, edited, designed, and produced by:

Book Creation Ltd., 20 Lochaline Street, London W6 9SH, United Kingdom

Managing Director: Hal Robinson

Editor: Alison Moore **Project Editor:** Marilyn Inglis **Art Editor:** Keith Miller

Designers: Michael Chapman, Austin Taylor; Evelyn Bercott **Copy Editor:** Sarah Barlow